An Ideal Husband

Oscar Wilde

W F HOWES LTD

This large print edition published in 2013 by
W F Howes Ltd
Unit 4, Rearsby Business Park, Gaddesby Lane,
Rearsby, Leicester LE7 4YH

1 3 5 7 9 10 8 6 4 2

First published in the United Kingdom in 1895
by L. Smithers

A CIP catalogue record for this book is available
from the British Library

ISBN 978 1 47122 896 4

Typeset by Palimpsest Book Production Limited,
Falkirk, Stirlingshire
Printed and bound in Great Britain
by MPG Books Ltd, Bodmin, Cornwall

MIX
Paper from
responsible sources
FSC® C018575

An Ideal Husband

ALSO BY OSCAR WILDE
FROM CLIPPER LARGE PRINT

The Picture of Dorian Gray

To
FRANK HARRIS
a slight tribute to his power and
distinction as an artist, his chivalry
and his nobility as a friend

PERSONS IN THE PLAY

THE EARL OF CAVERSHAM KG
VISCOUNT GORING, *his son*
SIR ROBERT CHILTERN BART, *Under-Secretary for Foreign Affairs*
VICOMTE DE NANJAC, *attaché at the French Embassy in London*
MR MONTFORD
MASON, *butler to Sir Robert Chiltern*
PHIPPS, *Lord Goring's servant*
JAMES, *footman*
HAROLD, *footman*
LADY CHILTERN
LADY MARKBY
THE COUNTESS OF BASILDON
MRS MARCHMONT
MISS MABEL CHILTERN, *Sir Robert Chiltern's sister*
MRS CHEVELEY

THE SCENES OF THE PLAY

ACT ONE   *The octagon room in Sir Robert Chiltern's house in Grosvenor Square*

ACT TWO   *The morning-room in Sir Robert Chiltern's house*

ACT THREE *The library of Lord Goring's house in Curzon Street*

ACT FOUR *Same as Act Two*

TIME: *The Present*

PLACE: *London*

The action of the play is completed within twenty-four hours

FIRST PERFORMANCE

Theatre Royal, Haymarket, London, on 3 January 1895

AN IDEAL HUSBAND

ACT ONE

The octagon room at Sir Robert Chiltern's house in Grosvenor Square. The room is brilliantly lighted and full of guests. At the top of the staircase stands LADY CHILTERN, *a woman of grave Greek beauty, about twenty-seven years of age. She receives the guests as they come up. Over the well of the staircase hangs a great chandelier with wax lights which illumine a large eighteenth-century French tapestry – representing the* Triumph of Love, *from a design by Boucher – that is stretched on the staircase wall. On the right is the entrance to the music-room. The sound of a string quartet is faintly heard. The entrance on the left leads to other reception rooms.* MRS MARCHMONT *and* LADY BASILDON, *two very pretty women, are seated together on a Louis-Seize sofa. They are types of exquisite fragility. Their affectation of manner has a delicate charm. Watteau would have loved to paint them.*

MRS MARCHMONT
  Going on to the Hartlocks, tonight, Margaret?

LADY BASILDON
  I suppose so. Are you?

MRS MARCHMONT
  Yes. Horribly tedious parties they give, don't they?

LADY BASILDON
  Horribly tedious! Never know why I go. Never know why I go anywhere.

MRS MARCHMONT
  I come here to be educated.

LADY BASILDON
  Ah! I hate being educated!

MRS MARCHMONT
  So do I. It puts one almost on a level with the commercial classes, doesn't it? But dear Gertrude Chiltern is always telling me that I should have some serious purpose in life. So I come here to try to find one.

LADY BASILDON (*looking round through her lorgnette*)
  I don't see anybody here tonight whom one could possibly call a serious purpose. The man who took me in to dinner talked to me about his wife the whole time.

MRS MARCHMONT
  How very trivial of him!

LADY BASILDON
Terribly trivial! What did your man talk about?

MRS MARCHMONT
About myself.

LADY BASILDON (*languidly*)
And were you interested?

MRS MARCHMONT (*shaking her head*)
Not in the smallest degree.

LADY BASILDON
What martyrs we are, dear Margaret!

MRS MARCHMONT (*rising*)
And how well it becomes us, Olivia!

They rise and go towards the music-room. The
VICOMTE DE NANJAC, *a young attaché known*
for his neckties and his Anglomania, approaches
with a low bow and enters into conversation

MASON
(*announcing guests from the top of the staircase*)
Mr and Lady Jane Barford. Lord Caversham.

Enter LORD CAVERSHAM, *an old gentleman of*
seventy, wearing the riband and star of the
Garter. A fine Whig type. Rather like a portrait
by Lawrence.

LORD CAVERSHAM
Good-evening, Lady Chiltern! Has my good-
for-nothing young son been here?

LADY CHILTERN (*smiling*)
I don't think Lord Goring has arrived yet.

MABEL CHILTERN (*coming up to* LORD CAVERSHAM)
Why do you call Lord Goring good-for-nothing?

> MABEL CHILTERN *is a perfect example of the
> English type of prettiness, the apple-blossom
> type. She has all the fragrance and freedom
> of a flower. There is ripple after ripple of
> sunlight in her hair, and the little mouth, with
> its parted lips, is expectant, like the mouth of
> a child. She has the fascinating tyranny of
> youth, and the astonishing courage of innocence.
> To sane people she is not reminiscent of any
> work of art. But she is really like a Tanagra
> statuette, and would be rather annoyed if she
> were told so.*

LORD CAVERSHAM
Because he leads such an idle life.

MABEL CHILTERN
How can you say such a thing? Why, he rides
in the Row at ten o'clock in the morning, goes to
the opera three times a week, changes his clothes
at least five times a day, and dines out every
night of the season. You don't call that leading
an idle life, do you?

LORD CAVERSHAM (*looking at her with a kindly
twinkle in his eyes*) You are a very charming young
lady!

MABEL CHILTERN

How sweet of you to say that, Lord Caversham! Do come to us more often. You know we are always at home on Wednesdays, and you look so well with your star!

LORD CAVERSHAM

Never go anywhere now. Sick of London society. Shouldn't mind being introduced to my own tailor; he always votes on the right side. But object strongly to being sent down to dinner with my wife's milliner. Never could stand Lady Caversham's bonnets.

MABEL CHILTERN

Oh, I love London society! I think it has immensely improved. It is entirely composed now of beautiful idiots and brilliant lunatics. Just what society should be.

LORD CAVERSHAM

Hum! Which is Goring? Beautiful idiot or the other thing?

MABEL CHILTERN (*gravely*)

I have been obliged for the present to put Lord Goring into a class quite by himself. But he is developing charmingly!

LORD CAVERSHAM

Into what?

MABEL CHILTERN (*with a little curtsey*)

I hope to let you know very soon, Lord Caversham!

MASON (*announcing guests*)
Lady Markby. Mrs Cheveley.

Enter LADY MARKBY *and* MRS CHEVELEY.
LADY MARKBY *is a pleasant, kindly, popular woman, with grey hair* à la marquise *and good lace.* MRS CHEVELEY, *who accompanies her, is tall and rather slight. Lips very thin and highly-coloured, a line of scarlet on a pallid face. Venetian red hair, aquiline nose and long throat. Rouge accentuates the natural paleness of her complexion. Grey-green eyes that move restlessly. She is in heliotrope, with diamonds. She looks rather like an orchid, and makes great demands on one's curiosity. In all her movements she is extremely graceful. A work of art, on the whole, but showing the influence of too many schools.*

LADY MARKBY
Good-evening, dear Gertrude! So kind of you to let me bring my friend Mrs Cheveley. Two such charming women should know each other!

LADY CHILTERN (*advances towards* MRS CHEVELEY *with a sweet smile. Then suddenly stops, and bows rather distantly*)
I think Mrs Cheveley and I have met before. I did not know she had married a second time.

LADY MARKBY (*genially*)
Ah, nowadays people marry as often as they can,

don't they? It is most fashionable. (*To* DUCHESS OF MARYBOROUGH)

Dear duchess, and how is the duke? Brain still weak, I suppose? Well, that is only to be expected, is it not? His good father was just the same. There is nothing like race, is there.

MRS CHEVELEY (*playing with her fan*)
But have we really met before, Lady Chiltern? I can't remember where. I have been out of England for so long.

LADY CHILTERN
We were at school together, Mrs Cheveley.

MRS CHEVELEY (*superciliously*)
Indeed? I have forgotten all about my school-days. I have a vague impression that they were detestable.

LADY CHILTERN (*coldly*)
I am not surprised!

MRS CHEVELEY (*in her sweetest manner*)
Do you know, I am quite looking forward to meeting your clever husband, Lady Chiltern. Since he has been at the Foreign Office, he has been so much talked of in Vienna. They actually succeed in spelling his name right in the news-papers. That in itself is fame, on the continent.

LADY CHILTERN
I hardly think there will be much in common

between you and my husband, Mrs Cheveley! (*moves away.*)

VICOMTE DE NANJAC

Ah, chère madame, quelle surprise! I have not seen you since Berlin!

MRS CHEVELEY

Not since Berlin, vicomte. Five years ago!

VICOMTE DE NANJAC

And you are younger and more beautiful than ever. How do you manage it?

MRS CHEVELEY

By making it a rule only to talk to perfectly charming people like yourself.

VICOMTE DE NANJAC

Ah! you flatter me. You butter me, as they say here.

MRS CHEVELEY

Do they say that here? How dreadful of them!

VICOMTE DE NANJAC

Yes, they have a wonderful language. It should be more widely known.

SIR ROBERT CHILTERN *enters. A man of forty but looking somewhat younger. Clean-shaven, with finely cut features, dark-haired and dark-eyed. A personality of mark. Not popular – few personalities are. But intensely admired by the few, and deeply respected by the many. The note of his manner is that of perfect distinction, with a slight touch of pride. One feels that he is conscious of the success he had made in life. A nervous temperament, with a tired look. The firmly chiselled mouth and chin contrast strikingly with the romantic expression in the deep-set eyes. The variance is suggestive of an almost complete separation of passion and intellect, as though thought and emotion were each isolated in its own sphere through some violence of willpower. There is nervousness in the nostrils, and in the pale, thin, pointed hands. It would be inaccurate to call him picturesque. Picturesqueness cannot survive the House of Commons. But Van Dyck would have liked to have painted his head.*

SIR ROBERT CHILTERN
Good-evening, Lady Markby. I hope you have brought Sir John with you?

LADY MARKBY
Oh! I have brought a much more charming person than Sir John. Sir John's temper since he has taken seriously to politics has become quite unbearable. Really, now that the House of Commons is trying to become useful, it does a great deal of harm.

SIR ROBERT CHILTERN
I hope not, Lady Markby. At any rate we do our best to waste the public time, don't we? But who

is this charming person you have been kind enough to bring to us?

LADY MARKBY

Her name is Mrs Cheveley! One of the Dorsetshire Cheveleys, I suppose. But I really don't know. Families are so mixed nowadays. Indeed, as a rule, everybody turns out to be somebody else.

SIR ROBERT CHILTERN

Mrs Cheveley? I seem to know the name.

LADY MARKBY

She has just arrived from Vienna.

SIR ROBERT CHILTERN

Ah! yes. I think I know whom you mean.

LADY MARKBY

Oh! she goes everywhere there, and has such pleasant scandals about all her friends. I really must go to Vienna next winter. I hope there is a good chef at the embassy.

SIR ROBERT CHILTERN

If there is not, the ambassador will certainly have to be recalled. Pray point out Mrs Cheveley to me. I should like to see her.

LADY MARKBY

Let me introduce you. (*To* MRS CHEVELEY.) My dear, Sir Robert Chiltern is dying to know you!

SIR ROBERT CHILTERN (*bowing*)

Everyone is dying to know the brilliant

Mrs Cheveley. Our attachés at Vienna write to us about nothing else.

MRS CHEVELEY

Thank you, Sir Robert. An acquaintance that begins with a compliment is sure to develop into a real friendship. It starts in the right manner. And I find that I know Lady Chiltern already.

SIR ROBERT CHILTERN

Really?

MRS CHEVELEY

Yes. She has just reminded me that we were at school together. I remember it perfectly now. She always got the good conduct prize. I have a distinct recollection of Lady Chiltern always getting the good conduct prize!

SIR ROBERT CHILTERN (*smiling*)

And what prizes did you get, Mrs Cheveley?

MRS CHEVELEY

My prizes came a little later on in life. I don't think any of them were for good conduct. I forget!

SIR ROBERT CHILTERN

I am sure they were for something charming!

MRS CHEVELEY

I don't know that women are always rewarded for being charming. I think they are usually punished for it! Certainly, more women grow old nowadays through the faithfulness of their admirers than through anything else! At least that is the only way I can account for the terribly haggard look of most of your pretty women in London!

SIR ROBERT CHILTERN

What an appalling philosophy that sounds! To attempt to classify you, Mrs Cheveley, would be an impertinence. But may I ask, at heart, are you an optimist or a pessimist? Those seem to be the only two fashionable religions left to us nowadays.

MRS CHEVELEY

Oh, I'm neither. Optimism begins in a broad grin, and Pessimism ends with blue spectacles. Besides, they are both of them merely poses.

SIR ROBERT CHILTERN

You prefer to be natural?

MRS CHEVELEY

Sometimes. But it is such a very difficult pose to keep up.

SIR ROBERT CHILTERN

What would those modern psychological novelists, of whom we hear so much, say to such a theory as that?

MRS CHEVELEY

Ah! the strength of women comes from the fact that psychology cannot explain us. Men can be analysed, women . . . merely adored.

SIR ROBERT CHILTERN

You think science cannot grapple with the problem of women?

MRS CHEVELEY

Science can never grapple with the irrational. That is why it has no future before it, in this world.

SIR ROBERT CHILTERN

And women represent the irrational.

MRS CHEVELEY

Well-dressed women do.

SIR ROBERT CHILTERN (*with a polite bow*)

I fear I could hardly agree with you there. But do sit down. And now tell me, what makes you leave your brilliant Vienna for our gloomy London – or perhaps the question is indiscreet?

MRS CHEVELEY

Questions are never indiscreet. Answers some-times are.

SIR ROBERT CHILTERN

Well, at any rate, may I know if it is politics or pleasure?

MRS CHEVELEY

Politics are my only pleasure. You see nowadays it is not fashionable to flirt till one is forty, or to be romantic till one is forty-five, so we poor women who are under thirty, or say we are, have nothing open to us but politics or philanthropy. And philanthropy seems to me to have become simply the refuge of people who wish to annoy their fellow creatures. I prefer politics. I think they are more . . . becoming!

SIR ROBERT CHILTERN
A political life is a noble career!

MRS CHEVELEY
Sometimes. And sometimes it is a clever game, Sir Robert. And sometimes it is a great nuisance.

SIR ROBERT CHILTERN
Which do you find it?

MRS CHEVELEY
A combination of all three. (*drops her fan*)

SIR ROBERT CHILTERN
(*picks up fan*)
Allow me!

MRS CHEVELEY
Thanks.

SIR ROBERT CHILTERN
But you have not told me yet what makes you honour London so suddenly. Our season is almost over.

MRS CHEVELEY
Oh! I don't care about the London season! It is too matrimonial. People are either hunting for husbands, or hiding from them. I wanted to meet

you. It is quite true. You know what a woman's curiosity is. Almost as great as a man's! I wanted immensely to meet you, and . . . to ask you to do something for me.

SIR ROBERT CHILTERN
I hope it is not a little thing, Mrs Cheveley. I find that little things are so very difficult to do.

MRS CHEVELEY (*after a moment's reflection*)
No, I don't think it is quite a little thing.

SIR ROBERT CHILTERN
I am so glad. Do tell me what it is.

MRS CHEVELEY
Later on. (*rises.*) And now may I walk through your beautiful house? I hear your pictures are charming. Poor Baron Arnheim – you remember the baron? – used to tell me you had some wonderful Corots.

SIR ROBERT CHILTERN (*with an almost imperceptible start*)
Did you know Baron Arnheim well?

MRS CHEVELEY (*smiling*)
Intimately. Did you?

SIR ROBERT CHILTERN
At one time.

MRS CHEVELEY
Wonderful man, wasn't he?

SIR ROBERT CHILTERN (*after a pause*)
He was very remarkable, in many ways.

MRS CHEVELEY
I often think it such a pity he never wrote his memoirs. They would have been most interesting.

SIR ROBERT CHILTERN
Yes he knew men and cities well, like the old Greek.

MRS CHEVELEY
Without the dreadful disadvantage of having a Penelope waiting at home for him.

MASON
Lord Goring.

Enter LORD GORING. *Thirty-four, but always says he is younger. A well-bred, expressionless face. He is clever, but would not like to be thought so. A flawless dandy, he would be annoyed if he were considered romantic. He plays with life, and is on perfectly good terms with the world. He is fond of being misunderstood. It gives him a post of vantage.*

SIR ROBERT CHILTERN
Good-evening, my dear Arthur! Mrs Cheveley, allow me to introduce to you Lord Goring, the idlest man in London.

MRS CHEVELEY
I have met Lord Goring before.

LORD GORING (*bowing*)
I did not think you would remember me, Mrs Cheveley.

MRS CHEVELEY
My memory is under admirable control. And are you still a bachelor?

LORD GORING
I . . . believe so.

MRS CHEVELEY
How very romantic!

LORD GORING
Oh! I am not at all romantic. I am not old enough. I leave romance to my seniors.

SIR ROBERT CHILTERN
Lord Goring is the result of Boodle's Club, Mrs Cheveley.

MRS CHEVELEY
He reflects every credit on the institution.

LORD GORING
May I ask are you staying in London long?

MRS CHEVELEY
That depends partly on the weather, partly on the cooking, and partly on Sir Robert.

SIR ROBERT CHILTERN
You are not going to plunge us into a European war, I hope?

MRS CHEVELEY
There is no danger, at present!

She nods to LORD GORING, *with a look of amusement in her eyes, and goes out with* SIR ROBERT CHILTERN. LORD GORING *saunters over to* MABEL CHILTERN.

MABEL CHILTERN
You are very late!

LORD GORING
Have you missed me?

MABEL CHILTERN
Awfully!

LORD GORING
Then I am sorry I did not stay away longer. I like being missed.

MABEL CHILTERN
How very selfish of you!

LORD GORING
I am very selfish.

MABEL CHILTERN
You are always telling me of your bad qualities, Lord Goring.

LORD GORING
I have only told you half of them as yet, Miss Mabel!

MABEL CHILTERN

Are the others very bad?

LORD GORING

Quite dreadful! When I think of them at night I go to sleep at once.

MABEL CHILTERN

Well, I delight in your bad qualities. I wouldn't have you part with one of them.

LORD GORING

How very nice of you! But then you are always nice. By the way, I want to ask you a question, Miss Mabel. Who brought Mrs Cheveley here? That woman in heliotrope, who has just gone out of the room with your brother?

MABEL CHILTERN

Oh, I think Lady Markby brought her. Why do you ask?

LORD GORING

I haven't seen her for years, that is all.

MABEL CHILTERN

What an absurd reason!

LORD GORING

All reasons are absurd.

MABEL CHILTERN

What sort of a woman is she?

LORD GORING

Oh! a genius in the daytime and a beauty at night!

MABEL CHILTERN

I dislike her already.

LORD GORING

That shows your admirable good taste.

VICOMTE DE NANJAC (*approaching*)

Ah, the English young lady is the dragon of good taste, is she not? Quite the dragon of good taste.

LORD GORING

So the newspapers are always telling us.

VICOMTE DE NANJAC

I read all your English newspapers. I find them so amusing.

LORD GORING

Then, my dear Nanjac, you must certainly read between the lines.

VICOMTE DE NANJAC

I should like to, but my professor objects. (*To* MABEL CHILTERN)
May I have the pleasure of escorting you to the music-room, mademoiselle?

MABEL CHILTERN (*looking very disappointed*)
Delighted, vicomte, quite delighted! (*Turning to* LORD GORING)
Aren't you coming to the music-room?

LORD GORING

Not if there is any music going on, Miss Mabel.

MABEL CHILTERN (*severely*)

The music is in German. You would not understand it.

Goes out with the VICOMTE DE NANJAC. LORD CAVERSHAM *comes up to his son*

LORD CAVERSHAM

Well, sir! what are you doing here? Wasting your life as usual! You should be in bed, sir. You keep too late hours! I heard of you the other night at Lady Rufford's dancing till four o'clock in the morning!

LORD GORING

Only a quarter to four, father.

LORD CAVERSHAM

Can't make out how you stand London society. The thing has gone to the dogs, a lot of damned nobodies talking about nothing.

LORD GORING

I love talking about nothing, father. It is the only thing I know anything about.

LORD CAVERSHAM

You seem to me to be living entirely for pleasure.

LORD GORING

What else is there to live for, father? Nothing ages like happiness.

LORD CAVERSHAM
You are heartless, sir, very heartless.

LORD GORING
I hope not, father. Good-evening, Lady Basildon!

LADY BASILDON (*arching two pretty eyebrows*)
Are you here? I had no idea you ever came to political parties.

LORD GORING
I adore political parties. They are the only place left to us where people don't talk politics.

LADY BASILDON
I delight in talking politics. I talk them all day long. But I can't bear listening to them. I don't know how the unfortunate men in the House stand these long debates.

LORD GORING
By never listening.

LADY BASILDON
Really?

LORD GORING (*in his most serious manner*)
Of course. You see, it is a very dangerous thing to listen. If one listens one may be convinced; and a man who allows himself to be convinced by an argument is a thoroughy unreasonable person.

LADY BASILDON
Ah! that accounts for so much in men that I

have never understood, and so much in women that their husbands never appreciate in them!

MRS MARCHMONT (*with a sigh*)
Our husbands never appreciate anything in us. We have to go to others for that!

LADY BASILDON (*emphatically*)
Yes, always to others, have we not?

LORD GORING (*smiling*)
And those are the views of the two ladies who are known to have the most admirable husbands in London.

MRS MARCHMONT
That is exactly what we can't stand. My Reginald is quite hopelessly faultless. He is really unendurably so, at times! There is not the smallest element of excitement in knowing him.

LORD GORING
How terrible! Really, the thing should be more widely known!

LADY BASILDON
Basildon is quite as bad; he is as domestic as if he was a bachelor.

MRS MARCHMONT (*pressing* LADY BASILDON'S *hand*)
My poor Olivia! We have married perfect husbands, and we are well punished for it.

LORD GORING

I should have thought it was the husbands who were punished.

MRS MARCHMONT (*drawing herself up*)
Oh, dear no! They are as happy as possible! And as for trusting us, it is tragic how much they trust us.

LADY BASILDON
Perfectly tragic!

LORD GORING
Or comic, Lady Basildon?

LADY BASILDON
Certainly not comic, Lord Goring. How unkind of you to suggest such a thing!

MRS MARCHMONT
I am afraid Lord Goring is in the camp of the enemy, as usual. I saw him talking to that Mrs Cheveley when he came in.

LORD GORING
Handsome woman, Mrs Cheveley!

LADY BASILDON (*stiffly*)
Please don't praise other women in our presence. You might wait for us to do that!

LORD GORING
I did wait.

MRS MARCHMONT
Well, we are not going to praise her. I hear she

went to the opera on Monday night, and told Tommy Rufford at supper that, as far as she could see, London society was entirely made up of dowdies and dandies.

LORD GORING
She is quite right, too. The men are all dowdies and the women are all dandies, aren't they?

MRS MARCHMONT (*after a pause*)
Oh! do you really think that is what Mrs Cheveley meant?

LORD GORING
Of course. And a very sensible remark for Mrs Cheveley to make, too.

Enter MABEL CHILTERN. *She joins the group*

MABEL CHILTERN
Why are you talking about Mrs Cheveley? Everybody is talking about Mrs Cheveley! Lord Goring, says – what did you say, Lord Goring about Mrs Cheveley? Oh! I remember, that she was a genius in the daytime and a beauty at night.

LADY BASILDON
What a horrid combination! So very unnatural!

MRS MARCHMONT (*in her most dreamy manner*)
I like looking at geniuses, and listening to beautiful people!

LORD GORING
Ah! that is morbid of you, Mrs Marchmont!

MRS MARCHMONT (*brightening to a look of real pleasure*)
I am so glad to hear you say that. Marchmont and I have been married for seven years, and he has never once told me that I was morbid. Men are so painfully unobservant.

LADY BASILDON (*turning to her*)
I have always said, dear Margaret, that you were the most morbid person in London.

MRS MARCHMONT
Ah! but you are always sympathetic, Olivia!

MABEL CHILTERN
Is it morbid to have a desire for food? I have a great desire for food. Lord Goring, will you give me some supper?

LORD GORING
With pleasure, Miss Mabel. (*moves away with her*)

MABEL CHILTERN
How horrid you have been! You have never talked to me the whole evening!

LORD GORING
How could I? You went away with the child-diplomatist.

MABEL CHILTERN
You might have followed us. Pursuit would have been only polite. I don't think I like you at all this evening!

LORD GORING

I like you immensely.

MABEL CHILTERN

Well, I wish you'd show it in a more marked way!

They go downstairs

MRS MARCHMONT

Olivia, I have a curious feeling of absolute faint-ness. I think I should like some supper very much. I know I should like some supper.

LADY BASILDON

I am positively dying for supper, Margaret!

MRS MARCHMONT

Men are so horribly selfish, they never think of these things.

LADY BASILDON

Men are grossly material, grossly material!

The VICOMTE DE NANJAC *enters from the music-room with some other guests. After having carefully examined all the people present, he approaches* LADY BASILDON

VICOMTE DE NANJAC

May I have the honour of taking you down to supper, Comtesse?

LADY BASILDON (*coldly*)

I never take supper, thank you, vicomte. (*The* VICOMTE DE NANJAC *is about to retire.* LADY BASILDON,

29

seeing this, rises at once and takes his arm) But I will come down with you with pleasure.

VICOMTE DE NANJAC
I am so fond of eating! I am very English in all my tastes.

LADY BASILDON
You look quite English, vicomte, quite English.

They pass out. MR MONTFORD, *a perfectly groomed young dandy, approaches* MRS MARCHMONT

MR MONTFORD
Like some supper, Mrs Marchmont?

MRS MARCHMONT (*languidly*)
Thank you, Mr Montford, I never touch supper. (*rises hastily and takes his arm*) But I will sit beside you, and watch you.

MR MONTFORD
I don't know that I like being watched when I am eating!

MRS MARCHMONT
Then I will watch someone else.

MR MONTFORD
I don't know that I should like that either.

MRS MARCHMONT (*severely*)
Pray, Mr Montford, do not make these painful scenes of jealousy in public!

They go downstairs with the other guests, passing
SIR ROBERT CHILTERN *and* MRS CHEVELEY,
who now enter

SIR ROBERT CHILTERN

And are you going to any of our country houses before you leave England, Mrs Cheveley?

MRS CHEVELEY

Oh, no! I can't stand your English house-parties. In England people actually try to be brilliant at breakfast. That is so dreadful of them! Only dull people are brilliant at breakfast. And then the family skeleton is always reading family prayers. My stay in England really depends on you, Sir Robert. (*sits down on the sofa*)

SIR ROBERT CHILTERN (*taking a seat beside her*)
Seriously?

MRS CHEVELEY

Quite seriously. I want to talk to you about a great political and financial scheme, about this Argentine Canal Company, in fact.

SIR ROBERT CHILTERN

What a tedious, practical subject for you to talk about, Mrs Cheveley!

MRS CHEVELEY

Oh, I like tedious, practical subjects. What I don't like are tedious, practical people. There is a wide difference. Besides, you are interested, I know, in international canal schemes. You were Lord

Radley's secretary, weren't you, when the government bought the Suez Canal shares?

SIR ROBERT CHILTERN

Yes. But the Suez Canal was a very great and splendid undertaking. It gave us our direct route to India. It had imperial value. It was necessary that we should have control. This Argentine scheme is a commonplace Stock Exchange swindle.

MRS CHEVELEY

A speculation, Sir Robert! A brilliant, daring speculation.

SIR ROBERT CHILTERN

Believe me, Mrs Cheveley, it is a swindle. Let us call things by their proper names. It makes matters simpler. We have all the information about it at the Foreign Office. In fact, I sent out a special commission to enquire into the matter privately, and they report that the works are hardly begun, and as for the money already subscribed, no one seems to know what has become of it. The whole thing is a second Panama, and with not a quarter of the chance of success that miserable affair ever had. I hope you have not invested in it. I am sure you are far too clever to have done that.

MRS CHEVELEY

I have invested very largely in it.

SIR ROBERT CHILTERN

Who could have advised you to do such a foolish thing?

MRS CHEVELEY

Your old friend – and mine.

SIR ROBERT CHILTERN

Who?

MRS CHEVELEY

Baron Arnheim.

SIR ROBERT CHILTERN (*frowning*)

Ah! yes. I remember hearing, at the time of his death, that he had been mixed up in the whole affair.

MRS CHEVELEY

It was his last romance. His last but one, to do him justice.

SIR ROBERT CHILTERN (*rising*)

But you have not seen my Corots yet. They are in the music-room. Corots seem to go with music, don't they? May I show them to you?

MRS CHEVELEY (*shaking her head*)

I am not in a mood tonight for silver twilights, or rose-pink dawns. I want to talk business. (*motions to him with her fan to sit down again beside her*)

SIR ROBERT CHILTERN

I fear I have no advice to give you, Mrs Cheveley,

except to interest yourself in something less dangerous. The success of the canal depends, of course, on the attitude of England, and I am going to lay the report of the commissioners before the House tomorrow night.

MRS CHEVELEY

That you must not do. In your own interests, Sir Robert, to say nothing of mine, you must not do that.

SIR ROBERT CHILTERN (*looking at her in wonder*)

In my own interests? My dear Mrs Cheveley, what do you mean? (*sits down beside her*)

MRS CHEVELEY

Sir Robert, I will be quite frank with you. I want you to withdraw the report that you had intended to lay before the House, on the ground that you have reasons to believe that the commissioners have been prejudiced, or misinformed, or something. Then I want you to say a few words to the effect that the government is going to reconsider the question, and that you have reason to believe that the canal, if completed, will be of great international value. You know the sort of things ministers say in cases of this kind. A few ordinary platitudes will do. In modern life nothing produces such an effect as a good platitude. It makes the whole world kin. Will you do that for me?

SIR ROBERT CHILTERN

Mrs Cheveley, you cannot be serious in making me such a proposition!

MRS CHEVELEY
I am quite serious.

SIR ROBERT CHILTERN (*coldly*)
Pray allow me to believe that you are not.

MRS CHEVELEY (*speaking with great deliberation and emphasis*)
Ah! but I am. And if you do what I ask you, I . . . will pay you very handsomely!

SIR ROBERT CHILTERN
Pay me!

MRS CHEVELEY
Yes.

SIR ROBERT CHILTERN
I am afraid I don't quite understand what you mean.

MRS CHEVELEY (*leaning back on the sofa and looking at him*)
How very disappointing! And I have come all the way from Vienna in order that you should thoroughly understand me.

SIR ROBERT CHILTERN
I fear I don't.

MRS CHEVELEY (*in her most nonchalant manner*)
My dear Sir Robert, you are a man of the world, and you have your price, I suppose. Everybody

has nowadays. The drawback is that most people are so dreadfully expensive. I know I am. I hope you will be more reasonable in your terms.

SIR ROBERT CHILTERN (*rises indignantly*)
If you will allow me, I will call your carriage for you. You have lived so long abroad, Mrs Cheveley, that you seem to be unable to realise that you are talking to an English gentleman.

MRS CHEVELEY (*detains him by touching his arm with her fan, and keeping it there while she is talking*)
I realise that I am talking to a man who laid the foundation of his fortune by selling to a Stock Exchange speculator a cabinet secret.

SIR ROBERT CHILTERN (*biting his lip*)
What do you mean?

MRS CHEVELEY (*rising and facing him*)
I mean that I know the real origin of your wealth and your career, and I have got your letter, too.

SIR ROBERT CHILTERN
What letter?

MRS CHEVELEY (*contemptuously*)
The letter you wrote to Baron Arnheim, when you were Lord Radley's secretary, telling the baron to buy Suez Canal shares – a letter written three days before the government announced its own purchase.

SIR ROBERT CHILTERN (*hoarsely*)

It is not true.

MRS CHEVELEY

You thought that letter had been destroyed.
How foolish of you! It is in my possession.

SIR ROBERT CHILTERN

The affair to which you allude was no more than
a speculation. The House of Commons had not
yet passed the bill; it might have been rejected.

MRS CHEVELEY

It was a swindle, Sir Robert. Let us call things
by their proper names. It makes everything
simpler. And now I am going to sell you that
letter, and the price I ask for it is your public
support of the Argentine scheme. You made your
own fortune out of one canal. You must help me
and my friends to make our fortunes out of
another!

SIR ROBERT CHILTERN

It is infamous, what you propose – infamous!

MRS CHEVELEY

Oh, no! This is the game of life as we all have
to play it, Sir Robert, sooner or later!

SIR ROBERT CHILTERN

I cannot do what you ask me.

MRS CHEVELEY

You mean you cannot help doing it. You know
you are standing on the edge of a precipice. And

it is not for you to make terms. It is for you to accept them. Supposing you refuse –

SIR ROBERT CHILTERN

What then?

MRS CHEVELEY

My dear Sir Robert, what then? You are ruined, that is all! Remember to what a point your puritanism in England has brought you. In the old days nobody pretended to be a bit better than his neighbours. In fact, to be a bit better than one's neighbours was considered excessively vulgar and middle-class. Nowadays, with our modern mania for morality, everyone has to pose as a paragon of purity, incorruptibility and all the other seven deadly virtues – and what is the result? You all go over like ninepins – one after the other. Not a year passes in England without somebody disappearing. Scandals used to lend charm, or at least interest, to a man – now they crush him. And yours is a very nasty scandal. You couldn't survive it. If it were known that as a young man, secretary to a great and important minister, you sold a cabinet secret for a large sum of money, and that was the origin of your wealth and career, you would be hounded out of public life, you would disappear completely. And after all, Sir Robert, why should you sacrifice your entire future rather than deal diplomatically with your enemy? For the moment I am your enemy. I admit it! And I am much stronger than you are. The big battalions are on my side. You have a splendid position, but it is your splendid position that makes you so vulnerable. You can't defend it! And I am in attack. Of course I have not talked morality to you. You must admit in fairness that I have spared you that. Years ago you did a clever, unscrupulous thing; it turned out a great success. You owe to it your fortune and position. And now you have got to pay for it. Sooner or later we have all to pay for what we do. You have to pay now. Before I leave you tonight, you have got to promise me to suppress your report, and to speak in the House in favour of this scheme.

SIR ROBERT CHILTERN
What you ask is impossible.

MRS CHEVELEY
You must make it possible. You are going to make it possible. Sir Robert, you know what your English newspapers are like. Suppose that when I leave this house I drive down to some newspaper office, and give them this scandal and the proofs of it! Think of their loathsome joy, of the delight they would have in dragging you down, of the mud and mire they would plunge you in. Think of the hypocrite with his greasy smile penning his leading article, and arranging the foulness of the public placard.

SIR ROBERT CHILTERN

Stop! You want me to withdraw the report and to make a short speech stating that I believe there are possibilities in the scheme?

MRS CHEVELEY (*sitting down on the sofa*)

Those are my terms.

SIR ROBERT CHILTERN (*in a low voice*)

I will give you any sum of money you want.

MRS CHEVELEY

Even you are not rich enough, Sir Robert, to buy back your past. No man is.

SIR ROBERT CHILTERN

I will not do what you ask me. I will not.

MRS CHEVELEY

You have to. If you don't . . . (*rises from the sofa*)

SIR ROBERT CHILTERN (*bewildered and unnerved*)

Wait a moment! What did you propose? You said that you would give me back my letter, didn't you?

MRS CHEVELEY

Yes. That is agreed. I will be in the Ladies' Gallery tomorrow night at half-past eleven. If by that time – and you will have had heaps of opportunity – you have made an announcement to the House in the terms I wish, I shall hand you back your letter with the prettiest thanks, and the best, or at any rate the most suitable, compliment I can think of. I intend to play quite fairly with you. One should always play fairly . . . when one has the winning cards. The baron taught me that . . . amongst other things.

SIR ROBERT CHILTERN

You must let me have time to consider your proposal.

MRS CHEVELEY

No; you must settle now!

SIR ROBERT CHILTERN

Give me a week – three days!

MRS CHEVELEY

Impossible! I have got to telegraph to Vienna tonight.

SIR ROBERT CHILTERN

My God! what brought you into my life?

MRS CHEVELEY

Circumstances. (*moves towards the door*)

SIR ROBERT CHILTERN

Don't go. I consent. The report shall be withdrawn. I will arrange for a question to be put to me on the subject.

MRS CHEVELEY

Thank you. I knew we should come to an amicable agreement. I understood your nature from the first. I analysed you, though you did not adore me. And now you can get my carriage for me, Sir Robert. I see the people coming up from supper, and Englishmen always get romantic after a meal, and that bores me dreadfully. (*Exit* SIR ROBERT CHILTERN.)

Enter LADY CHILTERN, LADY MARKBY, LORD CAVERSHAM, LADY BASILDON, MRS MARCH-MONT, VICOMTE DE NANJAC, MR MONTFORD

LADY MARKBY
Well, dear Mrs Cheveley, I hope you have enjoyed yourself. Sir Robert is very entertaining, is he not?

MRS CHEVELEY
Most entertaining! I have enjoyed my talk with him immensely.

LADY MARKBY
He has had a very interesting and brilliant career. And he has married a most admirable wife. Lady Chiltern is a woman of the very highest principles, I am glad to say. I am a little too old now myself, to trouble about setting a good example, but I always admire people who do. And Lady Chiltern has a very ennobling effect on life, though her dinner-parties are rather dull sometimes. But one can't have everything, can one? And now I must go, dear. Shall I call for you tomorrow?

MRS CHEVELEY
Thanks.

LADY MARKBY

We might drive in the park at five. Everything looks so fresh in the park now!

MRS CHEVELEY

Except the people!

LADY MARKBY

Perhaps the people are a little jaded. I have often observed that the season as it goes on produces a kind of softening of the brain. However, I think anything is better than high intellectual pressure. That is the most unbecoming thing there is. It makes the noses of the young girls so particularly large. And there is nothing so difficult to marry as a large nose; men don't like them. Good-night, dear! (*To* LADY CHILTERN)

Good-night, Gertrude! (*goes out on* LORD CAVERSHAM'S *arm*)

MRS CHEVELEY

What a charming house you have, Lady Chiltern! I have spent a delightful evening. It has been so interesting getting to know your husband.

LADY CHILTERN

Why did you wish to meet my husband, Mrs Cheveley?

MRS CHEVELEY

Oh, I will tell you. I wanted to interest him in this Argentine Canal Scheme, of which I dare say you have heard. And I found him most susceptible – susceptible to reason, I mean. A rare thing in a man. I converted him in ten minutes. He is going to make a speech in the House tomorrow night in favour of the idea. We must go to the Ladies' Gallery and hear him! It will be a great occasion!

LADY CHILTERN
There must be some mistake. That scheme could never have my husband's support.

MRS CHEVELEY
Oh, I assure you it's all settled. I don't regret my tedious journey from Vienna now. It has been a great success. But, of course, for the next twenty-four hours the whole thing is a dead secret.

LADY CHILTERN (*gently*)
A secret? Between whom?

MRS CHEVELEY (*with a flash of amusement in her eyes*)
Between your husband and myself.

SIR ROBERT CHILTERN (*entering*)
Your carriage is here, Mrs Cheveley!

MRS CHEVELEY
Thanks! Good-evening, Lady Chiltern! Good-night, Lord Goring! I am at Claridge's. Don't you think you might leave a card?

LORD GORING
If you wish it, Mrs Cheveley!

MRS CHEVELEY
Oh, don't be so solemn about it, or I shall be obliged to leave a card on you. In England I suppose that would hardly be considered *en règle*. Abroad, we are more civilised. Will you see me down, Sir Robert? Now that we have both the same interests at heart we shall be great friends, I hope!

Sails out on SIR ROBERT CHILTERN's *arm.* LADY CHILTERN *goes to the top of the staircase and looks down at them as they descend. Her expression is troubled. After a little time she is joined by some of the guests, and passes with them into another reception room.*

MABEL CHILTERN
What a horrid woman!

LORD GORING
You should go to bed, Miss Mabel.

MABEL CHILTERN
Lord Goring!

LORD GORING
My father told me to go to bed an hour ago. I don't see why I shouldn't give you the same advice. I always pass on good advice. It is the only thing to do with it. It is never of any use to oneself.

MABEL CHILTERN

Lord Goring, you are always ordering me out of the room. I think it most courageous of you. Especially as I am not going to bed for hours. (*goes over to the sofa*) You can come and sit down if you like, and talk about anything in the world, except the Royal Academy, Mrs Cheveley or novels in Scotch dialect. They are not improving subjects. (*catches sight of something that is lying on the sofa half-hidden by the cushion*) What is this? Someone has dropped a diamond brooch! Quite beautiful, isn't it? (*shows it to him*) I wish it was mine, but Gertrude won't let me wear anything but pearls, and I am thoroughly sick of pearls. They make one look so plain, so good and so intellectual. I wonder whom the brooch belongs to.

LORD GORING

I wonder who dropped it.

MABEL CHILTERN

It is a beautiful brooch.

LORD GORING

It is a handsome bracelet.

MABEL CHILTERN

It isn't a bracelet. It's a brooch.

LORD GORING

It can be used as a bracelet. (*takes it from her, and, pulling out a green letter-case, puts the ornament carefully in it, and replaces the whole thing in his breast-pocket with the most perfect* sang froid)

MABEL CHILTERN
What are you doing?

LORD GORING
Miss Mabel, I am going to make a rather strange request to you.

MABEL CHILTERN (*eagerly*)
Oh, pray do! I have been waiting for it all the evening.

LORD GORING (*is a little taken aback, but recovers himself*)
Don't mention to anybody that I have taken charge of this brooch. Should anyone write and claim it, let me know at once.

MABEL CHILTERN
That is a strange request.

LORD GORING
Well, you see I gave this brooch to somebody once, years ago.

MABEL CHILTERN
You did?

LORD GORING
Yes.

LADY CHILTERN *enters alone. The other guests have gone*

47

MABEL CHILTERN

  Then I shall certainly bid you good-night.
  Good-night, Gertrude! (*exit*)

LADY CHILTERN

  Good-night, dear! (*To* LORD GORING)
  You saw whom Lady Markby brought here
  tonight?

LORD GORING

  Yes. It was an unpleasant surprise. What did she
  come here for?

LADY CHILTERN

  Apparently to try and lure Robert to uphold
  some fraudulent scheme in which she is interested. The Argentine canal, in fact.

LORD GORING

  She has mistaken her man, hasn't she?

LADY CHILTERN

  She is incapable of understanding an upright
  nature like my husband's!

LORD GORING

  Yes. I should fancy she came to grief if she
  tried to get Robert into her toils. It is extraordinary what astounding mistakes clever women
  make.

LADY CHILTERN

  I don't call women of that kind clever. I call
  them stupid!

LORD GORING

Same thing often. Good-night, Lady Chiltern!

LADY CHILTERN

Good-night!

Enter SIR ROBERT CHILTERN

SIR ROBERT CHILTERN

My dear Arthur, you are not going? Do stop a little!

LORD GORING

Afraid I can't, thanks. I have promised to look in at the Hartlocks. I believe they have got a mauve Hungarian band that plays mauve Hungarian music. See you soon. Goodbye! (*exit*)

SIR ROBERT CHILTERN

How beautiful you look tonight, Gertrude!

LADY CHILTERN

Robert, it is not true, is it? You are not going to lend your support to this Argentine speculation? You couldn't!

SIR ROBERT CHILTERN (*starting*)

Who told you I intended to do so?

LADY CHILTERN

That woman who has just gone out, Mrs Cheveley, as she calls herself now. She seemed to taunt me with it. Robert, I know this woman. You don't. We were at school together. She was untruthful, dishonest, an evil influence on everyone whose trust or friendship she could win. I hated, I despised her. She stole things, she was a thief. She was sent away for being a thief. Why do you let her influence you?

SIR ROBERT CHILTERN

Gertrude, what you tell me may be true, but it happened many years ago. It is best forgotten! Mrs Cheveley may have changed since then. No one should be entirely judged by their past.

LADY CHILTERN (*sadly*)

One's past is what one is. It is the only way by which people should be judged.

SIR ROBERT CHILTERN

That is a hard saying, Gertrude!

LADY CHILTERN

It is a true saying, Robert. And what did she mean by boasting that she had got you to lend your support, your name, to a thing I have heard you describe as the most dishonest and fraudulent scheme there has ever been in political life?

SIR ROBERT CHILTERN (*biting his lip*)

I was mistaken in the view I took. We all may make mistakes.

LADY CHILTERN

But you told me yesterday that you had received the report from the commission, and that it entirely condemned the whole thing.

SIR ROBERT CHILTERN (*walking up and down*)
I have reasons now to believe that the commission was prejudiced, or, at any rate, misinformed. Besides, Gertrude, public and private life are different things. They have different laws, and move on different lines.

LADY CHILTERN
They should both represent man at his highest. I see no difference between them.

SIR ROBERT CHILTERN (*stopping*)
In the present case, on a matter of practical politics, I have changed my mind. That is all.

LADY CHILTERN
All!

SIR ROBERT CHILTERN (*sternly*)
Yes!

LADY CHILTERN
Robert! Oh! it is horrible that I should have to ask you such a question – Robert, are you telling me the whole truth?

SIR ROBERT CHILTERN
Why do you ask me such a question?

LADY CHILTERN (*after a pause*)
Why do you not answer it?

SIR ROBERT CHILTERN (*sitting down*)
Gertrude, truth is a very complex thing, and politics is a very complex business. There are

wheels within wheels. One may be under certain obligations to people that one must pay. Sooner or later in political life one has to compromise. Everyone does.

LADY CHILTERN

Compromise? Robert, why do you talk so differently tonight from the way I have always heard you talk? Why are you changed?

SIR ROBERT CHILTERN

I am not changed. But circumstances alter things.

LADY CHILTERN

Circumstances should never alter principles.

SIR ROBERT CHILTERN

But if I told you —

LADY CHILTERN

What?

SIR ROBERT CHILTERN

That it was necessary, vitally necessary?

LADY CHILTERN

It can never be necessary to do what is not honourable. Or if it be necessary, then what is it that I have loved! But it is not, Robert; tell me it is not. Why should it be? What gain would you get? Money? We have no need of that! And money that comes from a tainted source is a degradation. Power? But Power is nothing in itself. It is power to do good that is fine – that, and that only. What is it, then? Robert, tell me why you are going to do this dishonourable thing!

SIR ROBERT CHILTERN

Gertrude, you have no right to use that word. I told you it was a question of rational compromise. It is no more than that.

LADY CHILTERN

Robert, that is all very well for other men, for men who treat life simply as a sordid speculation; but not for you, Robert, not for you. You are different. All your life you have stood apart from others. You have never let the world soil you. To the world, as to myself, you have been an ideal always. Oh! be that ideal still. That great inheritance throw not away – that tower of ivory do not destroy. Robert, men can love what is beneath them – things unworthy, stained, dishonoured. We women worship when we love; and when we lose our worship, we lose everything. Oh! don't kill my love for you, don't kill that!

SIR ROBERT CHILTERN

Gertrude!

LADY CHILTERN

I know that there are men with horrible secrets in their lives – men who have done some shameful thing, and who in some critical moment have to

pay for it, by doing some other act of shame –
oh! don't tell me you are such as they are! Robert,
is there in your life any secret dishonour or
disgrace? Tell me, tell me at once, that –

SIR ROBERT CHILTERN
That what?

LADY CHILTERN (*speaking very slowly*)
That our lives may drift apart.

SIR ROBERT CHILTERN
Drift apart?

LADY CHILTERN
That they may entirely separate. It would be
better for us both.

SIR ROBERT CHILTERN
Gertrude, there is nothing in my past life that
you might not know.

LADY CHILTERN
I was sure of it, Robert, I was sure of it. But
why did you say those dreadful things, things so
unlike your real self? Don't let us ever talk about
the subject again. You will write, won't you, to
Mrs Cheveley, and tell her that you cannot
support this scandalous scheme of hers? If you
have given her any promise you must take it
back, that is all!

SIR ROBERT CHILTERN
Must I write and tell her that?

LADY CHILTERN

Surely, Robert! What else is there to do?

SIR ROBERT CHILTERN

I might see her personally. It would be better.

LADY CHILTERN

You must never see her again, Robert. She is not a woman you should ever speak to. She is not worthy to talk to a man like you. No; you must write to her at once, now, this moment, and let your letter show her that your decision is quite irrevocable!

SIR ROBERT CHILTERN

Write this moment!

LADY CHILTERN

Yes.

SIR ROBERT CHILTERN

But it is so late. It is close on twelve.

LADY CHILTERN

That makes no matter. She must know at once that she has been mistaken in you – and that you are not a man to do anything base or underhand or dishonourable. Write here, Robert. Write that you decline to support this scheme of hers, as you hold it to be a dishonest scheme. Yes – write the word dishonest. She knows what that word means. (SIR ROBERT CHILTERN *sits down and writes a letter. His wife takes it up and reads it.*)

Yes; that will do. (*rings bell*) And now the envelope. (*he writes the envelope slowly. Enter* MASON) Have this letter sent at once to Claridge's Hotel. There is no answer. (*exit* MASON. LADY CHILTERN *kneels down beside her husband and puts her arms around him*) Robert, love gives one an instinct to things. I feel tonight that I have saved you from something that might have been a danger to you, from something that might have made men honour you less than they do. I don't think you realise sufficiently, Robert, that you have brought into the political life of our time a nobler atmosphere, a finer attitude towards life, a freer air of purer aims and higher ideals – I know it, and for that I love you, Robert.

SIR ROBERT CHILTERN
Oh, love me always, Gertrude, love me always!

LADY CHILTERN
I will love you always, because you will always be worthy of love. We needs must love the highest when we see it! (*kisses him and rises and goes out*)

> SIR ROBERT CHILTERN *walks up and down for a moment; then sits down and buries his face in his hands. The servant enters and begins putting out the lights.* SIR ROBERT CHILTERN *looks up*

SIR ROBERT CHILTERN
Put out the lights, Mason, put out the lights!

The servant puts out the lights. The room becomes almost dark. The only light there is comes from the great chandelier that hangs over the staircase and illumines the tapestry of the Triumph of Love

END OF ACT ONE

ACT TWO

The morning-room at Sir Robert Chiltern's house. LORD GORING, *dressed in the height of fashion, is lounging in an armchair.* SIR ROBERT CHILTERN *is standing in front of the fireplace. He is evidently in a state of great mental excitement and distress. As the scene progresses he paces nervously up and down the room.*

LORD GORING

My dear Robert, it's a very awkward business, very awkward indeed. You should have told your wife the whole thing. Secrets from other people's wives are a necessary luxury in modern life. So, at least, I am always told at the club by people who are bald enough to know better. But no man should have a secret from his own wife. She invariably finds it out. Women have a wonderful instinct about things. They can discover everything except the obvious.

SIR ROBERT CHILTERN

Arthur, I couldn't tell my wife. When could I

have told her? Not last night. I would have made a life-long separation between us, and I would have lost the love of the one woman in the world I worship, of the only woman who has ever stirred love within me. Last night it would have been quite impossible. She would have turned from me in horror . . . in horror and in contempt.

LORD GORING
Is Lady Chiltern as perfect as all that?

SIR ROBERT CHILTERN
Yes; my wife is as perfect as all that.

LORD GORING (*taking off his left-hand glove*)
What a pity! I beg your pardon, my dear fellow, I didn't quite mean that. But if what you tell me is true, I should like to have a serious talk about life with Lady Chiltern.

SIR ROBERT CHILTERN
It would be quite useless.

LORD GORING
May I try?

SIR ROBERT CHILTERN
Yes, but nothing could make her alter her views.

LORD GORING
Well, at the worst it would simply be a psychological experiment.

SIR ROBERT CHILTERN
All such experiments are terribly dangerous.

LORD GORING

Everything is dangerous, my dear fellow. If it wasn't so, life wouldn't be worth living . . . Well, I am bound to say that I think you should have told her years ago.

SIR ROBERT CHILTERN

When? When we were engaged? Do you think she would have married me if she had known that the origin of my fortune is such as it is, the basis of my career such as it is, and that I had done a thing that I suppose most men would call shameful and dishonourable?

LORD GORING (*slowly*)

Yes; most men would call it ugly names. There is no doubt of that.

SIR ROBERT CHILTERN (*bitterly*)

Men who every day do something of the same kind themselves. Men who, each one of them, have worse secrets in their own lives.

LORD GORING

That is the reason they are so pleased to find out other people's secrets. It distracts public attention from their own.

SIR ROBERT CHILTERN

And, after all, whom did I wrong by what I did? No one.

LORD GORING (*looking at him steadily*)

Except yourself, Robert.

SIR ROBERT CHILTERN (*after a pause*)
Of course I had private information about a certain transaction contemplated by the government of the day, and I acted on it. Private information is practically the source of every large modern fortune.

LORD GORING (*tapping his boot with his cane*)
And public scandal invariably the result.

SIR ROBERT CHILTERN (*pacing up and down the room*)
Arthur, do you think that what I did nearly eighteen years ago should be brought up against me now? Do you think it fair that a man's whole career should be ruined for a fault done in his boyhood almost? I was twenty-two at the time, and I had the double misfortune of being well born and poor, two unforgivable things nowadays. Is it fair that the folly, the sin of one's youth, if men choose to call it a sin, should wreck a life like mine, should place me in the pillory, should shatter all that I have worked for, all that I have built up? Is it fair, Arthur?

LORD GORING
Life is never fair, Robert. And perhaps it is a good thing for most of us that it is not.

SIR ROBERT CHILTERN
Every man of ambition has to fight his century with its own weapons. What this century worships is wealth. The god of this century is wealth. To

succeed one must have wealth. At all costs one must have wealth.

LORD GORING

You underrate yourself, Robert. Believe me, without wealth you could have succeeded just as well.

SIR ROBERT CHILTERN

When I was old, perhaps. When I had lost my passion for power, or could not use it. When I was tired, worn out, disappointed. I wanted my success when I was young. Youth is the time for success. I couldn't wait.

LORD GORING

Well, you certainly have had your success while you are still young. No one in our day has had such a brilliant success. Under-Secretary for Foreign Affairs at the age of forty – that's good enough for anyone, I should think.

SIR ROBERT CHILTERN

And if it is all taken away from me now? If I lose everything over a horrible scandal? If I am hounded from public life?

LORD GORING

Robert, how could you have sold yourself for money?

SIR ROBERT CHILTERN (*excitedly*)

I did not sell myself for money. I bought success at a great price. That is all.

LORD GORING (*gravely*)
Yes; you certainly paid a great price for it. But what first made you think of doing such a thing?

SIR ROBERT CHILTERN
Baron Arnheim.

LORD GORING
Damned scoundrel!

SIR ROBERT CHILTERN
No; he was a man of a most subtle and refined intellect. A man of culture, charm, and distinction. One of the most intellectual men I ever met.

LORD GORING
Ah! I prefer a gentlemanly fool any day. There is more to be said for stupidity than people imagine. Personally I have a great admiration for stupidity. It is a sort of fellow-feeling, I suppose. But how did he do it? Tell me the whole thing.

SIR ROBERT CHILTERN (*throws himself into an armchair by the writing-table*)
One night after dinner at Lord Radley's the baron began talking about success in modern life as something that one could reduce to an absolutely definite science. With that wonderfully fascinating quiet voice of his he expounded to us the most terrible of all philosophies, the philosophy of power, preached to us the most marvellous of all gospels, the gospel of gold. I think he saw the effect he had produced on me,

for some days afterwards he wrote and asked me to come and see him. He was living then in Park Lane, in the house Lord Woolcomb has now. I remember so well how, with a strange smile on his pale, curved lips, he led me through his wonderful picture gallery, showed me his tapestries, his enamels, his jewels, his carved ivories, made me wonder at the strange loveliness of the luxury in which he lived; and then told me that luxury was nothing but a background, a painted scene in a play, and that power, power over other men, power over the world, was the one thing worth having, the one supreme pleasure worth knowing, the one joy one never tired of, and that in our century only the rich possessed it.

LORD GORING (*with great deliberation*)
A thoroughly shallow creed.

SIR ROBERT CHILTERN (*rising*)
I didn't think so then. I don't think so now. Wealth has given me enormous power. It gave me at the very outset of my life freedom, and freedom is everything. You have never been poor, and never known what ambition is. You cannot understand what a wonderful chance the baron gave me. Such a chance as few men get.

LORD GORING
Fortunately for them, if one is to judge by results. But tell me definitely, how did the baron finally persuade you to – well, to do what you did?

SIR ROBERT CHILTERN

When I was going away he said to me that if I ever could give him any private information of real value he would make me a very rich man. I was dazed at the prospect he held out to me, and my ambition and my desire for power were at that time boundless. Six weeks later certain private documents passed through my hands.

LORD GORING (*keeping his eyes steadily fixed on the carpet*)

State documents?

SIR ROBERT CHILTERN

Yes.

LORD GORING *sighs, then passes his hand across his forehead and looks up*

LORD GORING

I had no idea that you, of all men in the world, could have been so weak, Robert, as to yield to such a temptation as Baron Arnheim held out to you.

SIR ROBERT CHILTERN

Weak? Oh, I am sick of hearing that phrase. Sick of using it about others. Weak! Do you really think, Arthur, that it is weakness that yields to temptation? I tell you that there are terrible temptations that it requires strength, strength and courage, to yield to. To stake all one's life on a single moment, to risk everything on one throw, whether the stake be power or pleasure, I care not – there is no weakness in that. There is a horrible, a terrible courage. I had that courage. I sat down the same afternoon and wrote Baron Arnheim the letter this woman now holds. He made three-quarters of a million over the transaction.

LORD GORING
And you?

SIR ROBERT CHILTERN
I received from the baron a hundred and ten thousand pounds.

LORD GORING
You were worth more, Robert.

SIR ROBERT CHILTERN
No; that money gave me exactly what I wanted, power over others. I went into the House immediately. The baron advised me in finance from time to time. Before five years I had almost trebled my fortune. Since then everything that I have touched has turned out a success. In all things connected with money I have had a luck so extraordinary that sometimes it has made me almost afraid. I remember having read somewhere, in some strange book, that when the gods wish to punish us they answer our prayers.

LORD GORING

But tell me, Robert, did you never suffer any regret for what you had done?

SIR ROBERT CHILTERN

No. I felt that I had fought the century with its own weapons, and won.

LORD GORING (*sadly*)

You thought you had won.

SIR ROBERT CHILTERN

I thought so. (*after a long pause*) Arthur, do you despise me for what I have told you?

LORD GORING (*with deep feeling in his voice*)

I am very sorry for you, Robert, very sorry indeed.

SIR ROBERT CHILTERN

I don't say that I suffered any remorse. I didn't. Not remorse in the ordinary, rather silly sense of the word. But I have paid conscience money many times. I had a wild hope that I might disarm destiny. The sum Baron Arnheim gave me I have distributed twice over in public charities since then.

LORD GORING (*looking up*)

In public charities? Dear me! what a lot of harm you must have done, Robert!

SIR ROBERT CHILTERN

Oh, don't say that, Arthur; don't talk like that!

LORD GORING

Never mind what I say, Robert! I am always saying what I shouldn't say. In fact, I usually say what I really think. A great mistake nowadays. It makes one so liable to be understood. As regards this dreadful business, I will help you in whatever way I can. Of course you know that.

SIR ROBERT CHILTERN

Thank you, Arthur, thank you. But what is to be done? What can be done?

LORD GORING (*leaning back with his hands in his pockets*)

Well, the English can't stand a man who is always saying he is in the right, but they are very fond of a man who admits that he has been in the wrong. It is one of the best things in them. However, in your case, Robert, a confession would not do. The money, if you will allow me to say so, is . . . awkward. Besides, if you did make a clean breast of the whole affair, you would never be able to talk morality again. And in England a man who can't talk morality twice a week to a large, popular, immoral audience is quite over as a serious politician. There would be nothing left for him as a profession except botany or the church. A confession would be of no use. It would ruin you.

SIR ROBERT CHILTERN

It would ruin me. Arthur, the only thing for me to do now is to fight the thing out.

LORD GORING (*rising from his chair*)

I was waiting for you to say that, Robert. It is the only thing to do now. And you must begin by telling your wife the whole story.

SIR ROBERT CHILTERN

That I will not do.

LORD GORING

Robert, believe me, you are wrong.

SIR ROBERT CHILTERN

I couldn't do it. It would kill her love for me. And now about this woman, this Mrs Cheveley. How can I defend myself against her? You knew her before, Arthur, apparently.

LORD GORING

Yes.

SIR ROBERT CHILTERN

Did you know her well?

LORD GORING (*arranging his necktie*)

So little that I got engaged to be married to her once, when I was staying at the Tenbys. The affair lasted for three days . . . nearly.

SIR ROBERT CHILTERN

Why was it broken off?

LORD GORING (*airily*)

Oh, I forget. At least, it makes no matter. By the way, have you tried her with money? She used to be confoundedly fond of money.

SIR ROBERT CHILTERN

I offered her any sum she wanted. She refused.

LORD GORING

Then the marvellous gospel of gold breaks down sometimes. The rich can't do everything, after all.

SIR ROBERT CHILTERN

Not everything. I suppose you are right. Arthur, I feel that public disgrace is in store for me. I feel certain of it. I never knew what terror was before. I know it now. It is as if a hand of ice were laid upon one's heart. It is as if one's heart were beating itself to death in some empty hollow.

LORD GORING (*striking the table*)

Robert, you must fight her. You must fight her.

SIR ROBERT CHILTERN

But how?

LORD GORING

I can't tell you how at present. I have not the smallest idea. But everyone has some weak point. There is some flaw in each one of us. (*strolls over to the fireplace and looks at himself in the glass*) My father tells me that even I have faults. Perhaps I have. I don't know.

SIR ROBERT CHILTERN

In defending myself against Mrs Cheveley, I have a right to use any weapon I can find, have I not?

LORD GORING (*still looking in the glass*)

In your place I don't think I should have the smallest scruple in doing so. She is thoroughly well able to take care of herself.

SIR ROBERT CHILTERN (*sits down at the table and takes a pen in his hand*)

Well, I shall send a cipher telegram to the embassy at Vienna, to enquire if there is anything known against her. There may be some secret scandal she might be afraid of.

LORD GORING (*settling his buttonhole*)

Oh, I should fancy Mrs Cheveley is one of those very modern women of our time who find a new scandal as becoming as a new bonnet, and air them both in the park every afternoon at five-thirty. I am sure she adores scandals, and that the sorrow of her life at present is that she can't manage to have enough of them.

SIR ROBERT CHILTERN (*writing*)

Why do you say that?

LORD GORING (*turning round*)

Well, she wore far too much rouge last night,

and not quite enough clothes. That is always a sign of despair in a woman.

SIR ROBERT CHILTERN (*striking a bell*)
But it is worthwhile my wiring to Vienna, is it not?

LORD GORING
It is always worthwhile asking a question, though it is not always worthwhile answering one.

Enter MASON

SIR ROBERT CHILTERN
Is Mr Trafford in his room?

MASON
Yes, Sir Robert.

SIR ROBERT CHILTERN (*puts what he has written into an envelope, which he then carefully closes*)

Tell him to have this sent off in cipher at once. There must not be a moment's delay.

MASON
Yes, Sir Robert.

SIR ROBERT CHILTERN
Oh! just give that back to me again.

Writes something on the envelope. MASON *then goes out with the letter*

SIR ROBERT CHILTERN
She must have had some curious hold over Baron Arnheim. I wonder what it was.

LORD GORING (*smiling*)
  I wonder.

SIR ROBERT CHILTERN
  I will fight her to the death, as long as my wife
  knows nothing.

LORD GORING (*strongly*)
  Oh, fight in any case – in any case.

SIR ROBERT CHILTERN (*with a gesture of despair*)
  If my wife found out, there would be little left
  to fight for. Well, as soon as I hear from Vienna,
  I shall let you know the result. It is a chance,
  just a chance, but I believe in it. And as I fought
  the age with its own weapons, I will fight her
  with her weapons. It is only fair, and she looks
  like a woman with a past, doesn't she?

LORD GORING
  Most pretty women do. But there is a fashion
  in pasts just as there is a fashion in frocks.
  Perhaps Mrs Cheveley's past is merely a slightly
  décolleté one, and they are excessively popular
  nowadays. Besides, my dear Robert, I should
  not build too high hopes on frightening
  Mrs Cheveley. I should not fancy Mrs Cheveley
  is a woman who would be easily frightened. She
  has survived all her creditors, and she shows
  wonderful presence of mind.

SIR ROBERT CHILTERN
  Oh! I live on hopes now. I clutch at every chance.

I feel like a man on a ship that is sinking. The water is round my feet, and the very air is bitter with storm. Hush! I hear my wife's voice.

Enter LADY CHILTERN *in walking dress*

LADY CHILTERN
Good-afternoon, Lord Goring.

LORD GORING
Good-afternoon, Lady Chiltern! Have you been in the park?

LADY CHILTERN
No; I have just come from the Woman's Liberal Association, where, by the way, Robert, your name was received with loud applause, and now I have come in to have my tea. (*To* LORD GORING) You will wait and have some tea, won't you?

LORD GORING
I'll wait for a short time, thanks.

LADY CHILTERN
I will be back in a moment. I am only going to take my hat off.

LORD GORING (*in his most earnest manner*)
Oh! please don't. It is so pretty. One of the prettiest hats I ever saw. I hope the Woman's Liberal Association received it with loud applause.

LADY CHILTERN (*with a smile*)
We have much more important work to do than look at each other's bonnets, Lord Goring.

LORD GORING
Really? What sort of work?

LADY CHILTERN
Oh! dull, useful, delightful things, Factory Acts, Female Inspectors, the Eight Hours Bill, the Parliamentary Franchise . . . Everything in fact, that you would find thoroughly uninteresting.

LORD GORING
And never bonnets?

LADY CHILTERN (*with mock indignation*)
Never bonnets, never!

> LADY CHILTERN *goes out through the door leading to her boudoir*

SIR ROBERT CHILTERN (*takes* LORD GORING'S *hand*)
You have been a good friend to me, Arthur, a thoroughly good friend.

LORD GORING
I don't know that I have been able to do much for you, Robert, as yet. In fact, I have not been able to do anything for you, as far as I can see. I am thoroughly disappointed with myself.

SIR ROBERT CHILTERN
You have enabled me to tell you the truth. That is something. The truth has always stifled me.

LORD GORING
Ah! The truth is a thing I get rid of as soon as possible! Bad habit, by the way. Makes one

very unpopular at the club . . . with the older members. They call it being conceited. Perhaps it is.

SIR ROBERT CHILTERN

I would to God that I had been able to tell the truth . . . to live the truth. Ah! that is the great thing in life, to live the truth. (*sighs, and goes towards the door*) I'll see you soon again, Arthur, shan't I?

LORD GORING

Certainly. Whenever you like. I'm going to look in at the Bachelors' Ball tonight, unless I find something better to do. But I'll come round tomorrow morning. If you should want me tonight by any chance, send round a note to Curzon Street.

SIR ROBERT CHILTERN

Thank you.

As he reaches the door, LADY CHILTERN *enters from her boudoir*

LADY CHILTERN

You are not going, Robert?

SIR ROBERT CHILTERN

I have some letters to write, dear.

LADY CHILTERN (*going to him*)

You work too hard, Robert. You seem never to think of yourself, and you are looking so tired.

SIR ROBERT CHILTERN

It is nothing, dear, nothing. (*he kisses her and goes out*)

LADY CHILTERN (*to* LORD GORING)

Do sit down. I am so glad you have called. I want to talk to you about . . . well, not about bonnets, or the Woman's Liberal Association. You take far too much interest in the first subject; and not nearly enough in the second.

LORD GORING

You want to talk to me about Mrs Cheveley?

LADY CHILTERN

Yes. You have guessed it. After you left last night I found out that what she had said was really true. Of course I made Robert write her a letter at once, withdrawing his promise.

LORD GORING

So he gave me to understand.

LADY CHILTERN

To have kept it would have been the first stain on a career that has been stainless always. Robert must be above reproach. He is not like other men. He cannot afford to do what other men do. (*she looks at* LORD GORING, *who remains silent*) Don't you agree with me? You are Robert's greatest friend. You are our greatest friend, Lord Goring. No one, except myself, knows Robert better than you do. He has no secrets from me, and I don't think he has any from you.

78

LORD GORING

He certainly has no secrets from me. At least I don't think so.

LADY CHILTERN

Then am I not right in my estimate of him? I know I am right. But speak to me frankly.

LORD GORING (*looking straight at her*)
Quite frankly?

LADY CHILTERN

Surely. You have nothing to conceal, have you?

LORD GORING

Nothing. But, my dear Lady Chiltern, I think, if you will allow me to say so, that in practical life –

LADY CHILTERN (*smiling*)
Of which you know so little, Lord Goring –

LORD GORING

Of which I know nothing by experience, though I know something by observation. I think that in practical life there is something about success, actual success, that is a little unscrupulous, something about ambition that is unscrupulous always. Once a man has set his heart and soul on getting to a certain point, if he has to climb the crag, he climbs the crag; if he has to walk in the mire –

LADY CHILTERN

Well?

LORD GORING

He walks in the mire. Of course I am only talking generally about life.

LADY CHILTERN (*gravely*)

I hope so. Why do you look at me so strangely, Lord Goring?

LORD GORING

Lady Chiltern, I have sometimes thought that . . . perhaps you are a little hard in some of your views on life. I think that . . . often you don't make sufficient allowances. In every nature there are elements of weakness, or worse than weakness. Supposing, for instance, that – that any public man, my father, or Lord Merton, or Robert, say, had, years ago, written some foolish letter to someone . . .

LADY CHILTERN

What do you mean by a foolish letter?

LORD GORING

A letter gravely compromising one's position. I am only putting an imaginary case.

LADY CHILTERN

Robert is as incapable of doing a foolish thing as he is of doing a wrong thing.

LORD GORING (*after a long pause*)

Nobody is incapable of doing a foolish thing. Nobody is incapable of doing a wrong thing.

LADY CHILTERN

Are you a Pessimist? What will the other dandies say? They will all have to go into mourning.

LORD GORING (*rising*)

No, Lady Chiltern, I am not a Pessimist. Indeed I am not sure that I quite know what pessimism really means. All I do know is that life cannot be understood without much charity, cannot be lived without much charity. It is love, and not German philosophy, that is the true explanation of this world, whatever may be the explanation of the next. And if you are ever in trouble, Lady Chiltern, trust me absolutely, and I will help you in every way I can. If you ever want me, come to me for my assistance, and you shall have it. Come at once to me.

LADY CHILTERN (*looking at him in surprise*)

Lord Goring, you are talking quite seriously. I don't think I ever heard you talk seriously before.

LORD GORING (*laughing*)

You must excuse me, Lady Chiltern. It won't occur again, if I can help it.

LADY CHILTERN

But I like you to be serious.

Enter MABEL CHILTERN, *in the most ravishing frock*

MABEL CHILTERN

Dear Gertrude, don't say such a dreadful thing

to Lord Goring. Seriousness would be very unbecoming to him. Good-afternoon, Lord Goring! Pray be as trivial as you can.

LORD GORING
I should like to, Miss Mabel, but I am afraid I am . . . a little out of practice this morning; and, besides, I have to be going now.

MABEL CHILTERN
Just when I have come in! What dreadful manners you have! I am sure you were very badly brought up.

LORD GORING
I was.

MABEL CHILTERN
I wish I had brought you up!

LORD GORING
I am so sorry you didn't.

MABEL CHILTERN
It is too late now, I suppose?

LORD GORING (*smiling*)
I am not so sure.

MABEL CHILTERN
Will you ride tomorrow morning?

LORD GORING
Yes, at ten.

MABEL CHILTERN
Don't forget.

LORD GORING
Of course I shan't. By the way, Lady Chiltern, there is no list of your guests in the *Morning Post* of today. It has apparently been crowded out by the County Council, or the Lambeth Conference, or something equally boring. Could you let me have a list? I have a particular reason for asking you.

LADY CHILTERN
I am sure Mr Trafford will be able to give you one.

LORD GORING
Thanks, so much.

MABEL CHILTERN
Tommy is the most useful person in London.

LORD GORING (*turning to her*)
And who is the most ornamental?

MABEL CHILTERN (*triumphantly*)
I am.

LORD GORING
How clever of you to guess it! (*takes up his hat and cane*) Goodbye, Lady Chiltern! You will remember what I said to you, won't you?

LADY CHILTERN
Yes; but I don't know why you said it to me.

LORD GORING
I hardly know myself. Goodbye, Miss Mabel!

MABEL CHILTERN (*with a little moue of disappointment*)
I wish you were not going. I have had four wonderful adventures this morning, four and a half, in fact. You might stop and listen to some of them.

LORD GORING
How very selfish of you to have four and a half! There won't be any left for me.

MABEL CHILTERN
I don't want you to have any. They would not be good for you.

LORD GORING
That is the first unkind thing you have ever said to me. How charmingly you said it! Ten tomorrow.

MABEL CHILTERN
Sharp.

LORD GORING
Quite sharp. But don't bring Mr Trafford.

MABEL CHILTERN (*with a little toss of the head*)
Of course I shan't bring Tommy Trafford. Tommy Trafford is in great disgrace.

LORD GORING
I am delighted to hear it. (*bows and goes out*)

MABEL CHILTERN

Gertrude, I wish you would speak to Tommy Trafford.

LADY CHILTERN

What has poor Mr Trafford done this time? Robert says he is the best secretary he has ever had.

MABEL CHILTERN

Well, Tommy has proposed to me again. Tommy really does nothing but propose to me. He proposed to me last night in the music-room, when I was quite unprotected as there was an elaborate trio going on. I didn't dare to make the smallest repartee, I need hardly tell you. If I had, it would have stopped the music at once. Musical people are so absurdly unreasonable. They always want one to be perfectly dumb at the very moment when one is longing to be absolutely deaf. Then he proposed to me in broad daylight this morning, in front of that dreadful statue of Achilles. Really, the things that go on in front of that work of art are quite appalling. The police should interfere. At luncheon I saw by the glare in his eye that he was going to propose again, and I just managed to check him in time by assuring him that I was a bimetallist. Fortunately I don't know what bimetallism means. And I don't believe anybody else does either. But the observation crushed Tommy for ten minutes. He looked quite shocked.

And then Tommy is so annoying in the way he proposes. If he proposed at the top of his voice, I should not mind so much. That might produce some effect on the public. But he does it in a horrid confidential way. When Tommy wants to be romantic he talks to one just like a doctor. I am very fond of Tommy, but his methods of proposing are quite out of date. I wish, Gertrude, you would speak to him, and tell him that once a week is quite often enough to propose to anyone, and that it should always be done in a manner that attracts some attention.

LADY CHILTERN
Dear Mabel, don't talk like that. Besides, Robert thinks very highly of Mr Trafford. He believes he has a brilliant future before him.

MABEL CHILTERN
Oh! I wouldn't marry a man with a future before him for anything under the sun.

LADY CHILTERN
Mabel!

MABEL CHILTERN
I know, dear. You married a man with a future, didn't you? But then Robert was a genius, and you have a noble, self-sacrificing character. You can stand geniuses. I have no character at all, and Robert is the only genius I could ever bear. As a rule, I think they are quite impossible. Geniuses talk so much, don't they? Such a bad

habit! And they are always thinking about themselves, when I want them to be thinking about me. I must go round now and rehearse at Lady Basildon's. You remember, we are having tableaux, don't you? The Triumph of something, I don't know what! I hope it will be triumph of me. Only triumph I am really interested in at present. (*kisses* LADY CHILTERN *and goes out; then comes running back*) Oh, Gertrude, do you know who is coming to see you? That dreadful Mrs Cheveley, in a most lovely gown. Did you ask her?

LADY CHILTERN (*rising*)
Mrs Cheveley! Coming to see me? Impossible!

MABEL CHILTERN
I assure you she is coming upstairs as large as life and not nearly so natural.

LADY CHILTERN
You need not wait, Mabel. Remember, Lady Basildon is expecting you.

MABEL CHILTERN
Oh! I must shake hands with Lady Markby. She is delightful. I love being scolded by her.

Enter MASON

MASON
Lady Markby. Mrs Cheveley.

Enter LADY MARKBY *and* MRS CHEVELEY

LADY CHILTERN (*advancing to meet them*)
Dear Lady Markby, how nice of you to come and see me! (*shakes hands with her, and bows somewhat distantly to* MRS CHEVELEY) Won't you sit down, Mrs Cheveley?

MRS CHEVELEY
Thanks. Isn't that Miss Chiltern? I should like so much to know her.

LADY CHILTERN
Mabel, Mrs Cheveley wishes to know you. (MABEL CHILTERN *gives a little nod*)

MRS CHEVELEY (*sitting down*)
I thought your frock so charming last night, Miss Chiltern. So simple and . . . suitable.

MABEL CHILTERN
Really? I must tell my dressmaker. It will be such a surprise to her. Goodbye, Lady Markby!

LADY MARKBY
Going already?

MABEL CHILTERN
I am so sorry but I am obliged to. I am just off to rehearsal. I have got to stand on my head in some tableaux.

LADY MARKBY
On your head, child? Oh! I hope not. I believe it is most unhealthy. (*takes a seat on the sofa next to* LADY CHILTERN)

MABEL CHILTERN

But it is for an excellent charity in aid of the Undeserving, the only people I am really interested in. I am the secretary, and Tommy Trafford is treasurer.

MRS CHEVELEY

And what is Lord Goring?

MABEL CHILTERN

Oh! Lord Goring is president.

MRS CHEVELEY

The post should suit him admirably, unless he has deteriorated since I knew him first.

LADY MARKBY (*reflecting*)

You are remarkably modern, Mabel. A little too modern, perhaps. Nothing is so dangerous as being too modern. One is apt to grow old-fashioned quite suddenly. I have known many instances of it.

MABEL CHILTERN

What a dreadful prospect!

LADY MARKBY

Ah! my dear, you need not be nervous. You will always be as pretty as possible. That is the best fashion there is, and the only fashion that England succeeds in setting.

MABEL CHILTERN (*with a curtsey*)

Thank you so much, Lady Markby, for England . . . and myself. (*goes out*)

LADY MARKBY (*turning to* LADY CHILTERN)

Dear Gertrude, we just called to know if Mrs Cheveley's diamond brooch has been found.

LADY CHILTERN

Here?

MRS CHEVELEY

Yes. I missed it when I got back to Claridge's, and I thought I might possibly have dropped it here.

LADY CHILTERN

I have heard nothing about it. But I will send for the butler and ask. (*touches the bell*)

MRS CHEVELEY

Oh, pray don't trouble, Lady Chiltern. I dare say I lost it at the opera, before we came on here.

LADY MARKBY

Ah yes, I suppose it must have been at the opera. The fact is, we all scramble and jostle so much nowadays that I wonder we have anything at all left on us at the end of an evening. I know myself that, when I am coming back from the drawing room, I always feel as if I hadn't a shred on me, except a small shred of decent reputation, just enough to prevent the lower classes making painful observations through the windows of the carriage. The fact is that our society is terribly over-populated. Really, someone should arrange a proper scheme of assisted emigration. It would do a great deal of good.

MRS CHEVELEY
I quite agree with you, Lady Markby. It is nearly six years since I have been in London for the season, and I must say society has become dreadfully mixed. One sees the oddest people everywhere.

LADY MARKBY
That is quite true, dear. But one needn't know them. I'm sure I don't know half the people who come to my house. Indeed, from all I hear, I shouldn't like to.

Enter MASON

LADY CHILTERN
What sort of a brooch was it that you lost, Mrs Cheveley?

MRS CHEVELEY
A diamond snake-brooch with a ruby, a rather large ruby.

LADY MARKBY
I thought you said there was a sapphire on the head, dear?

MRS CHEVELEY (*smiling*)
No, Lady Markby – a ruby.

LADY MARKBY (*nodding her head*)
And very becoming, I am quite sure.

LADY CHILTERN

Has a ruby and diamond brooch been found in any of the rooms this morning, Mason?

MASON

No, my lady.

MRS CHEVELEY

It really is of no consequence, Lady Chiltern. I am so sorry to have put you to any inconvenience.

LADY CHILTERN (*coldly*)

Oh, it has been no inconvenience. That will do, Mason. You can bring tea. (*Exit* MASON.)

LADY MARKBY

Well, I must say it is most annoying to lose anything. I remember once at Bath, years ago, losing in the Pump Room an exceedingly handsome cameo bracelet that Sir John had given me. I don't think he has ever given me anything since, I am sorry to say. He has sadly degenerated. Really, this horrid House of Commons quite ruins our husbands for us. I think the Lower House by far the greatest blow to a happy married life that there has been since that terrible thing called the Higher Education of Women was invented.

LADY CHILTERN

Ah! it is heresy to say that in this house, Lady Markby. Robert is a great champion of the

Higher Education of Woman, and so, I am afraid, am I.

MRS CHEVELEY

The higher education of men is what I should like to see. Men need it so sadly.

LADY MARKBY

They do, dear. But I am afraid such a scheme would be quite unpractical. I don't think man has much capacity for development. He has got as far as he can, and that is not far, is it? With regard to women, well, dear Gertrude, you belong to the younger generation, and I am sure it is all right if you approve of it. In my time, of course, we were taught not to understand anything. That was the old system, and wonderfully interesting it was. I assure you that the amount of things I and my poor dear sister were taught not to understand was quite extraordinary. But modern women understand everything, I am told.

MRS CHEVELEY

Except their husbands. That is the one thing the modern woman never understands.

LADY MARKBY

And a very good thing too, dear, I dare say. It might break up many a happy home if they did. Not yours, I need hardly say, Gertrude. You have married a pattern husband. I wish I could say as much for myself. But since Sir

John has taken to attending the debates regularly, which he never used to do in the good old days, his language has become quite impossible. He always seems to think that he is addressing the House, and consequently whenever he discusses the state of the agricultural labourer, or the Welsh church, or something quite improper of that kind, I am obliged to send all the servants out of the room. It is not pleasant to see one's own butler, who has been with one for twenty-three years, actually blushing at the sideboard, and the footmen making contortions in corners like persons in circuses. I assure you my life will be quite ruined unless they send John at once to the Upper House. He won't take any interest in politics then, will he? The House of Lords is so sensible. An assembly of gentlemen. But in his present state, Sir John is really a great trial. Why, this morning before breakfast was half over, he stood up on the hearth-rug, put his hands in his pockets, and appealed to the country at the top of his voice. I left the table as soon as I had had my second cup of tea, I need hardly say. But his violent language could be heard all over the house! I trust, Gertrude, that Sir Robert is not like that?

LADY CHILTERN
But I am very much interested in politics, Lady Markby. I love to hear Robert talk about them.

LADY MARKBY

Well, I hope he is not as devoted to Blue Books as Sir John is. I don't think they can be quite improving reading for anyone.

MRS CHEVELEY (*languidly*)

I have never read a Blue Book. I prefer books . . . in yellow covers.

LADY MARKBY (*genially unconscious*)

Yellow is a gayer colour, is it not? I used to wear yellow a good deal in my early days, and would do so now if Sir John was not so painfully personal in his observations, and a man on the question of dress is always ridiculous, is he not?

MRS CHEVELEY

Oh, no! I think men are the only authorities on dress.

LADY MARKBY

Really? One wouldn't say so from the sort of hats they wear, would one?

THE BUTLER *enters, followed by* THE FOOTMAN. *Tea is set on a small table close to* LADY CHILTERN

LADY CHILTERN

May I give you some tea, Mrs Cheveley.

MRS CHEVELEY

Thanks. (THE BUTLER *hands* MRS CHEVELEY *a cup of tea on a salver*)

LADY CHILTERN

Some tea, Lady Markby?

LADY MARKBY

No thanks, dear. (THE SERVANTS *go out*) The fact is, I have promised to go round for ten minutes to see poor Lady Brancaster, who is in very great trouble. Her daughter, quite a well-brought-up girl, too, has actually become engaged to be married to a curate in Shropshire. It is very sad, very sad indeed. I can't understand this modern mania for curates. In my time we girls saw them, of course, running about the place like rabbits. But we never took any notice of them, I need hardly say. But I am told that nowadays country society is quite honeycombed with them. I think it most irreligious. And then the eldest son has quarrelled with his father, and it is said that when they meet at the club Lord Brancaster always hides himself behind the money article in *The Times*. However, I believe that is quite a common occurrence nowadays and that they have to take in extra copies of *The Times* at all the clubs in St James's Street, there are so many sons who won't have anything to do with their fathers, and so many fathers who won't speak to their sons. I think, myself, it is very much to be regretted.

MRS CHEVELEY

So do I. Fathers have so much to learn from their sons nowadays.

LADY MARKBY

Really, dear? What?

MRS CHEVELEY

The art of living. The only really fine art we have
produced in modern times.

LADY MARKBY (*shaking her head*)

Ah! I am afraid Lord Brancaster knew a good
deal about that. More than his poor wife ever
did. (*Turning to* LADY CHILTERN) You know Lady
Brancaster, don't you, dear?

LADY CHILTERN

Just slightly. She was staying at Langton last
autumn, when we were there.

LADY MARKBY

Well, like all stout women, she looks the very
picture of happiness, as no doubt you noticed.
But there are many tragedies in her family,
besides this affair of the curate. Her own sister,
Mrs Jekyll, had a most unhappy life; through no
fault of her own, I am sorry to say. She ultimately
was so broken-hearted that she went into a
convent, or on to the operatic stage, I forget
which. No; I think it was decorative art-needlework
she took up. I know she had lost all sense of
pleasure in life. (*Rising*) And now, Gertrude,
if you will allow me, I shall leave Mrs Cheveley
in your charge and call back for her in a quarter
of an hour. Or perhaps, dear Mrs Cheveley, you
wouldn't mind waiting in the carriage while I

am with Lady Brancaster. As I intend it to be a visit of condolence, I shan't stay long.

MRS CHEVELEY (*rising*)
I don't mind waiting in the carriage at all, provided there is somebody to look at one.

LADY MARKBY
Well, I hear the curate is always prowling about the house.

MRS CHEVELEY
I am afraid I am not fond of girl friends.

LADY CHILTERN (*rising*)
Oh, I hope Mrs Cheveley will stay here a little. I should like to have a few minutes' conversation with her.

MRS CHEVELEY
How very kind of you, Lady Chiltern! Believe me, nothing would give me greater pleasure.

LADY MARKBY
Ah! no doubt you both have many pleasant reminiscences of your schooldays to talk over together. Goodbye, dear Gertrude! Shall I see you at Lady Bonar's tonight? She has discovered a wonderful new genius. He does . . . nothing at all, I believe. That is a great comfort, is it not?

LADY CHILTERN
Robert and I are dining at home by ourselves tonight, and I don't think I shall go anywhere

afterwards. Robert, of course, will have to be in the House. But there is nothing interesting on.

LADY MARKBY

Dining at home by yourselves? Is that quite prudent? Ah, I forgot, your husband is an exception. Mine is the general rule, and nothing ages a woman so rapidly as having married the general rule.

Exit LADY MARKBY

MRS CHEVELEY

Wonderful woman, Lady Markby, isn't she? Talks more and says less than anybody I ever met. She is made to be a public speaker. Much more so than her husband, though he is a typical Englishman, always dull and usually violent.

LADY CHILTERN (*makes no answer, but remains standing. There is a pause. Then the eyes of the two women meet.* LADY CHILTERN *looks stern and pale.* MRS CHEVELEY *seems rather amused*)

Mrs Cheveley, I think it is right to tell you quite frankly that, had I known who you really were, I should not have invited you to my house last night.

MRS CHEVELEY (*with an impertinent smile*)
Really?

LADY CHILTERN

I could not have done so.

MRS CHEVELEY
I see that after all these years you have not changed a bit, Gertrude.

LADY CHILTERN
I never change.

MRS CHEVELEY (*elevating her eyebrows*)
Then life has taught you nothing?

LADY CHLTERN
It has taught me that a person who has once been guilty of a dishonest and dishonourable action may be guilty of it a second time, and should be shunned.

MRS CHEVELEY
Would you apply that rule to everyone?

LADY CHILTERN
Yes, to everyone, without exception.

MRS CHEVELEY
Then I am sorry for you, Gertrude, very sorry for you.

LADY CHILTERN
You see now, I am sure, that for many reasons any further acquaintance between us during your stay in London is quite impossible?

MRS CHEVELEY (*leaning back in her chair*)
Do you know, Gertrude, I don't mind your talking morality a bit. Morality is simply the attitude we adopt towards people whom we

100

personally dislike. You dislike me. I am quite aware of that. And I have always detested you. And yet I have come here to do you a service.

LADY CHILTERN (*contemptuously*)
Like the service you wished to render my husband last night, I suppose. Thank heaven, I saved him from that.

MRS CHEVELEY (*starting to her feet*)
It was you who made him write that insolent letter to me? It was you who made him break his promise?

LADY CHILTERN
Yes.

MRS CHEVELEY
Then you must make him keep it. I give you till tomorrow morning – no more. If by that time your husband does not solemnly bind himself to help me in this great scheme in which I am interested –

LADY CHILTERN
This fraudulent speculation –

MRS CHEVELEY
Call it what you choose. I hold your husband in the hollow of my hand, and if you are wise you will make him do what I tell him.

LADY CHILTERN (*rising and going towards her*)
You are impertinent. What has my husband to do with you? With a woman like you?

MRS CHEVELEY (*with a bitter laugh*)

In this world like meets with like. It is because your husband is himself fraudulent and dishonest that we pair so well together. Between you and him there are chasms. He and I are closer than friends. We are enemies linked together. The same sin binds us.

LADY CHILTERN

How dare you class my husband with yourself? How dare you threaten him or me? Leave my house. You are unfit to enter it.

> SIR ROBERT CHILTERN *enters from behind. He hears his wife's last words, and sees to whom they are addressed. He grows deadly pale.*

MRS CHEVELEY

Your house! A house bought with the price of dishonour. A house, everything in which has been paid for by fraud. (*turns round and sees* SIR ROBERT CHILTERN) Ask him what the origin of his fortune is! Get him to tell you how he sold to a stockbroker a cabinet secret. Learn from him to what you owe your position.

LADY CHILTERN

It is not true! Robert! It is not true!

MRS CHEVELEY (*pointing at him with outstretched finger*)

Look at him! Can he deny it? Does he dare to?

SIR ROBERT CHILTERN

Go! Go at once. You have done your worst now.

MRS CHEVELEY

My worst? I have not yet finished with you, with either of you. I give you both till tomorrow at noon. If by then you don't do what I bid you to do, the whole world shall know the origin of Robert Chiltern.

SIR ROBERT CHILTERN *strikes the bell. Enter* MASON

SIR ROBERT CHILTERN

Show Mrs Cleveley out.

MRS CHEVELEY *starts; then bows with somewhat exaggerated politeness to* LADY CHILTERN, *who makes no sign of response. As she passes by* SIR ROBERT CHILTERN, *who is standing close to the door, she pauses for a moment and looks him straight in the face. She then goes out, followed by the servant, who closes the door after him. The husband and wife are left alone.* LADY CHILTERN *stands like someone in a dreadful dream. Then she turns round and looks at her husband. She looks at him with strange eyes, as though she was seeing him for the first time.*

LADY CHILTERN

You sold a cabinet secret for money! You began your life with fraud! You built up your career

103

on dishonour! Oh, tell me it is not true! Lie to me! Lie to me! Tell me it is not true.

SIR ROBERT CHILTERN

What this woman said is quite true. But, Gertrude, listen to me. You don't realise how I was tempted. Let me tell you the whole thing. (*goes towards her*)

LADY CHILTERN

Don't come near me. Don't touch me. I feel as if you had soiled me for ever. Oh! what a mask you have been wearing all these years! A horrible painted mask! You sold yourself for money. Oh! a common thief were better. You put yourself up for sale to the highest bidder! You were bought in the market. You lied to the whole world. And yet you will not lie to me.

SIR ROBERT CHILTERN (*rushing towards her*)
Gertrude! Gertrude!

LADY CHILTERN (*thrusting him back with outstretched hands*)
No, don't speak! Say nothing! Your voice wakes terrible memories – memories of things that made me love you – memories of words that made me love you – memories that now are horrible to me. And how I worshipped you! You were to me something apart from common life, a thing pure, noble, honest, without stain. The world seemed to me finer because you were in it, and goodness more real because you lived.

And now – oh, when I think that I made of a man like you my ideal! the ideal of my life!

SIR ROBERT CHILTERN

There was your mistake. There was your error. The error all women commit. Why can't you women love us, faults and all? Why do you place us on monstrous pedestals? We have all feet of clay, women as well as men; but when we men love women, we love them knowing their weaknesses, their follies, their imperfections, love them all the more, it may be, for that reason. It is not the perfect, but the imperfect, who have need of love. It is when we are wounded by our own hands, or by the hands of others, that love should come to cure us – else what use is love at all? All sins, except a sin against itself, love should forgive. All lives, save loveless lives, true love should pardon. A man's love is like that. It is wider, larger, more human than a woman's. Women think that they are making ideals of men. What they are making of us are false idols merely. You made your false idol of me, and I had not the courage to come down, show you my wounds, tell you my weaknesses. I was afraid that I might lose your love, as I have lost it now. And so, last night you ruined my life for me – yes, ruined it! What this woman asked of me was nothing compared to what she offered to me. She offered security, peace, stability. The sin of my youth, that I had thought was buried, rose up in front of me, hideous, horrible, with its hands at my throat. I could have killed it for ever, sent it back into its tomb, destroyed its record, burned the one witness against me. You prevented me. No one but you, you know it. And now what is there before me but public disgrace, ruin, terrible shame, the mockery of the world, a lonely dishonoured life – a lonely dishonoured death, it may be, someday? Let women make no more ideals of men! let them not put them on altars and bow before them, or they may ruin other lives as completely as you – you whom I have so wildly loved – have ruined mine!

He passes from the room. LADY CHILTERN *rushes towards him, but the door is closed when she reaches it. Pale with anguish, bewildered, helpless, she sways like a plant in the water. Her hands, outstretched, seem to tremble in the air like blossoms in the wind. Then she flings herself down beside a sofa and buries her face. Her sobs are like the sobs of a child.*

 END OF ACT TWO

ACT THREE

The liberary in Lord Goring's house. An Adam room. On the right is the door leading into the hall. On the left, the door of the smoking-room. A pair of folding doors at the back open into the drawing-room. The fire is lit. PHIPPS, *the butler, is arranging some newspapers on the writing-table. The distinction of Phipps is his impassivity. He has been termed by enthusiasts the Ideal Butler. The Sphinx is not so incommunicable. He is a mask with a manner. Of his intellectual or emotional life, history knows nothing. He represents the dominance of form.*

Enter LORD GORING *in evening dress with a buttonhole. He is wearing a silk hat and Inverness cape. White-gloved, he carries a Louis-Seize cane. His are all the delicate fopperies of fashion. One sees that he stands in immediate relation to modern life, makes it indeed, and so masters it. He is the first well-dressed philosopher in the history of thought.*

LORD GORING

Got my second buttonhole for me, Phipps?

PHIPPS

Yes, my lord. (*takes his hat, cane and cape, and presents new buttonhole on salver*)

LORD GORING

Rather distinguished thing, Phipps. I am the only person of the smallest importance in London at present who wears a buttonhole.

PHIPPS

Yes, my lord. I have observed that.

LORD GORING (*taking out old buttonhole*)

You see, Phipps, fashion is what one wears oneself. What is unfashionable is what other people wear.

PHIPPS

Yes, my lord.

LORD GORING

Just as vulgarity is simply the conduct of other people.

PHIPPS

Yes, my lord.

LORD GORING (*putting in new buttonhole*)

And falsehoods the truths of other people.

PHIPPS

Yes, my lord.

LORD GORING

Other people are quite dreadful. The only possible society is oneself.

PHIPPS

Yes, my lord.

LORD GORING

To love oneself is the beginning of a lifelong romance, Phipps.

PHIPPS

Yes, my lord.

LORD GORING (*looking at himself in the glass*)

Don't think I quite like this buttonhole, Phipps. Makes me look a little too old. Makes me almost in the prime of life, eh, Phipps?

PHIPPS

I don't observe any alteration in your lordship's appearance.

LORD GORING

You don't, Phipps?

PHIPPS

No, my lord.

LORD GORING

I am not quite sure. For the future a more trivial buttonhole, Phipps, on Thursday evenings.

PHIPPS

I will speak to the florist, my lord. She has had

a loss in her family lately, which perhaps accounts for the lack of trivality your lordship complains of in the buttonhole.

LORD GORING

Extraordinary thing about the lower classes in England – they are always losing their relations.

PHIPPS

Yes, my lord! They are extremely fortunate in that respect.

LORD GORING (*turns round and looks at him.* PHIPPS *remains impassive*)

Hum! Any letters, Phipps?

PHIPPS

Three, my lord. (*hands letters on a salver*)

LORD GORING (*takes letters*)

Want my cab round in twenty minutes.

PHIPPS

Yes, my lord. (*goes towards door*)

LORD GORING (*holds up letter in pink envelope*)

Ahem, Phipps, when did this letter arrive?

PHIPPS

It was brought by hand just after your lordship went to the club.

LORD GORING

That will do. (*Exit* PHIPPS) Lady Chiltern's handwriting on Lady Chiltern's pink notepaper. That is rather curious. I thought Robert was to write. Wonder what Lady Chiltern has got to say to me? (*sits at bureau, opens letter and reads it*) 'I want you. I trust you. I am coming to you. Gertrude.' (*puts down the letter with a puzzled look; then takes it up, and reads it again slowly*) 'I want you. I trust you. I am coming to you.' So she has found out everything! Poor woman! Poor woman! (*pulls out watch and looks at it*) But what an hour to call! Ten o'clock! I shall have to give up going to the Berkshires. However, it is always nice to be expected, and not to arrive. I am not expected at the Bachelors', so I shall certainly go there. Well, I will make her stand by her husband. That is the only thing for any woman to do. It is the growth of the moral sense in women that makes marriage such a hopeless, one-sided institution. Ten o'clock. She should be here soon. I must tell Phipps I am not in to anyone else. (*goes towards bell*)

Enter PHIPPS

PHIPPS
Lord Caversham.

LORD GORING
Oh, why will parents always appear at the wrong time? Some extraordinary mistake in nature, I suppose. (*enter* LORD CAVERSHAM) Delighted to see you, my dear father. (*goes to meet him*)

LORD CAVERSHAM
Take my cloak off.

LORD GORING
Is it worthwhile, father?

LORD CAVERSHAM
Of course it is worthwhile, sir. Which is the most comfortable chair?

LORD GORING
This one, father. It is the chair I use myself, when I have visitors.

LORD CAVERSHAM
Thank ye. No draught, I hope, in this room?

LORD GORING
No, father.

LORD CAVERSHAM (*sitting down*)
Glad to hear it. Can't stand draughts. No draughts at home.

LORD GORING
Good many breezes, father.

LORD CAVERSHAM
Eh? Eh? Don't understand what you mean. Want to have a serious conversation with you, sir.

LORD GORING
My dear father! At this hour?

LORD CAVERSHAM
Well, sir, it is only ten o'clock. What is your

objection to the hour? I think the hour is an admirable hour!

LORD GORING
Well, the fact is, father, this is not my day for talking seriously. I am very sorry, but it is not my day.

LORD CAVERSHAM
What do you mean, sir?

LORD GORING
During the season, father, I only talk seriously on the first Tuesday in every month, from four to seven.

LORD CAVERSHAM
Well, make it Tuesday, sir, make it Tuesday.

LORD GORING
But it is after seven, father, and my doctor says I must not have any serious conversation after seven. It makes me talk in my sleep.

LORD CAVERSHAM
Talk in your sleep, sir? What does that matter? You are not married.

LORD GORING
No, father, I am not married.

LORD CAVERSHAM
Hum! That is what I have come to talk to you about, sir. You have got to get married, and at once. Why, when I was your age, sir, I had been

an inconsolable widower for three months and was already paying my addresses to your admirable mother. Damme, sir, it is your duty to get married. You can't be always living for pleasure. Every man of position is married nowadays. Bachelors are not fashionable any more. They are a damaged lot. Too much is known about them. You must get a wife, sir. Look where your friend Robert Chiltern has got to by probity, hard work and a sensible marriage with a good woman. Why don't you imitate him, sir? Why don't you take him for your model?

LORD GORING
I think I shall, father.

LORD CAVERSHAM
I wish you would, sir. Then I should be happy. At present I make your mother's life miserable on your account. You are heartless, sir, quite heartless.

LORD GORING
I hope not, father.

LORD CAVERSHAM
And it is high time for you to get married. You are thirty-four years of age, sir.

LORD GORING
Yes, father, but I only admit to thirty-two – thirty-one and a half when I have a really good

buttonhole. This buttonhole is not . . . trivial enough.

LORD CAVERSHAM

I tell you you are thirty-four, sir. And there is a draught in your room, besides, which makes your conduct worse. Why did you tell me there was no draught, sir? I feel a draught, sir, I feel it distinctly.

LORD GORING

So do I, father. It is a dreadful draught. I will come and see you tomorrow, father. We can talk over anything you like. Let me help you on with your cloak, father.

LORD CAVERSHAM

No, sir; I have called this evening for a definite purpose, and I am going to see it through at all costs to my health or yours. Put down my cloak, sir.

LORD GORING

Certainly, father. But let us go into another room. (*rings bell*) There is a dreadful draught here. (*Enter* PHIPPS) Phipps, is there a good fire in the smoking-room?

PHIPPS

Yes, my lord.

LORD GORING

Come in there, father. Your sneezes are quite heartrending.

LORD CAVERSHAM
Well, sir, I suppose I have a right to sneeze when I choose?

LORD GORING (*apologetically*)
Quite so, father. I was merely expressing sympathy.

LORD CAVERSHAM
Oh, damn sympathy. There is a great deal too much of that sort of thing going on nowadays.

LORD GORING
I quite agree with you, father. If there was less sympathy in the world there would be less trouble in the world.

LORD CAVERSHAM (*going towards the smoking-room*)
That is a paradox, sir. I hate paradoxes.

LORD GORING
So do I, father. Everybody one meets is a paradox nowadays. It is a great bore. It makes society so obvious.

LORD CAVERSHAM (*turning round, and looking at his son beneath his bushy eyebrows*)
Do you always really understand what you say, sir?

LORD GORING (*after some hesitation*)
Yes, father, if I listen attentively.

LORD CAVERSHAM (*indignantly*)
If you listen attentively! . . . Conceited young puppy!

Goes out grumbling into the smoking-room.
PHIPPS *enters*

LORD GORING
Phipps, there is a lady coming to see me this evening on particular business. Show her into the drawing-room when she arrives. You understand?

PHIPPS
Yes, my lord.

LORD GORING
It is a matter of the gravest importance, Phipps.

PHIPPS
I understand, my lord.

LORD GORING
No one else is to be admitted, under any circumstances.

PHIPPS
I understand, my lord. (*Bell rings*)

LORD GORING
Ah! that is probably the lady. I shall see her myself.

Just as he is going towards the door LORD CAVERSHAM *enters from the smoking-room*

LORD CAVERSHAM
Well, sir? am I to wait attendance on you?

LORD GORING (*considerably perplexed*)
In a moment, father. Do excuse me. (LORD

CAVERSHAM *goes back*) Well, remember my instructions, Phipps – into that room.

PHIPPS

Yes, my lord.

LORD GORING *goes into the smoking-room*

HAROLD, *the footman, shows* MRS CHEVELEY *in. Lamialike, she is in green and silver. She has a cloak of black satin, lined with dead rose-leaf silk.*

HAROLD

What name, madam?

MRS CHEVELEY (*to* PHIPPS, *who advances towards her*)

Is Lord Goring not here? I was told he was at home?

PHIPPS

His lordship is engaged at present with Lord Caversham, madam. (*turns a cold, glassy eye on* HAROLD, *who at once retires*)

MRS CHEVELEY (*to herself*)

How very filial!

PHIPPS

His lordship told me to ask you, madam, to be kind enough to wait in the drawing-room for him. His lordship will come to you there.

MRS CHEVELEY (*with a look of surprise*)

Lord Goring expects me?

PHIPPS

Yes, madam.

MRS CHEVELEY

Are you quite sure?

PHIPPS

His lordship told me that if a lady called I was to ask her to wait in the drawing-room. (*goes to the door of the drawing-room and opens it*) His lordship's directions on the subject were very precise.

MRS CHEVELEY (*to herself*)

How thoughtful of him! To expect the unexpected shows a thoroughly modern intellect. (*goes towards the drawing-room and looks in*) Ugh! How dreary a bachelor's drawing-room always looks. I shall have to alter all this. (PHIPPS *brings the lamp from the writing-table.*) No, I don't care for that lamp. It is far too glaring. Light some candles.

PHIPPS (*replaces lamp*)

Certainly, madam.

MRS CHEVELEY

I hope the candles have very becoming shades.

PHIPPS

We have had no complaints about them, madam, as yet.

Passes into the drawing-room and begins to light the candles

MRS CHEVELEY (*to herself*)

I wonder what woman he is waiting for tonight. It will be delightful to catch him. Men always look so silly when they are caught. And they are always being caught. (*Looks about room and approaches the writing-table*) What a very interesting room! What a very interesting picture! Wonder what his correspondence is like. (*takes up letters*) Oh, what a very uninteresting correspondence! Bills and cards, debts and dowagers! Who on earth writes to him on pink paper? How silly to write on pink paper! It looks like the beginning of a middle-class romance. Romance should never begin with sentiment. It should begin with science and end with a settlement. (*puts letter down, then takes it up again*) I know that handwriting. That is Gertrude Chiltern's. I remember it perfectly. The ten commandments in every stroke of the pen, and the moral law all over the page. Wonder what Gertrude is writing to him about? Something horrid about me, I suppose. How I detest that woman! (*reads it*) 'I trust you. I want you. I am coming to you. Gertrude.' 'I trust you. I want you. I am coming to you.'

A look of triumph comes over her face. She is just about to steal the letter, when PHIPPS *comes in*

PHIPPS

The candles in the drawing-room are lit, madam, as you directed.

MRS CHEVELEY

Thank you. (*rises hastily and slips the letter under a large silver-cased blotting-book that is lying on the table*)

PHIPPS

I trust the shades will be to your liking, madam. They are the most becoming we have. They are the same as his lordship uses himself when he is dressing for dinner.

MRS CHEVELEY (*with a smile*)

Then I am sure they will be perfectly right.

PHIPPS (*gravely*)

Thank you, madam.

> MRS CHEVELEY *goes into the drawing-room.* PHIPPS *closes the door and retires. The door is then slowly opened, and* MRS CHEVELEY *comes out and creeps stealthily towards the writing-table. Suddenly voices are heard from the smoking-room.* MRS CHEVELEY *grows pale, and stops. The voices grow louder, and she goes back into the drawing-room, biting her lip.*

> *Enter* LORD GORING *and* LORD CAVERSHAM

LORD GORING (*expostulating*)

My dear father, if I am to get married, surely you will allow me to choose the time, place and person? Particularly the person.

LORD CAVERSHAM (*testily*)

That is a matter for me, sir. You would probably make a very poor choice. It is I who should be consulted, not you. There is property at stake. It is not a matter for affection. Affection comes later on in married life.

LORD GORING

Yes. In married life affection comes when people thoroughly dislike each other, father, doesn't it? (*puts on* LORD CAVERSHAM's *cloak for him*)

LORD CAVERSHAM

Certainly, sir. I mean certainly not, sir. You are talking very foolishly tonight. What I say is that marriage is a matter for common sense.

LORD GORING

But women who have common sense are so curiously plain, father, aren't they? Of course I only speak from hearsay.

LORD CAVERSHAM

No woman, plain or pretty, has any common sense at all, sir. Common sense is the privilege of our sex.

LORD GORING

Quite so. And we men are so self-sacrificing that we never use it, do we, father?

LORD CAVERSHAM

I use it, sir. I use nothing else.

LORD GORING

So my mother tells me.

LORD CAVERSHAM

It is the secret of your mother's happiness. You are very heartless, sir, very heartless.

LORD GORING

I hope not, father.

Goes out for a moment. Then returns, looking rather put out, with SIR ROBERT CHILTERN

SIR ROBERT CHILTERN

My dear Arthur, what a piece of good luck meeting you on the doorstep! Your servant had just told me you were not at home. How extraordinary!

LORD GORING

The fact is, I am horribly busy tonight, Robert, and I gave orders I was not at home to anyone. Even my father had a comparatively cold reception. He complained of a draught the whole time.

SIR ROBERT CHILTERN

Ah! you must be at home to me, Arthur. You are my best friend. Perhaps by tomorrow you will be my only friend. My wife has discovered everything.

LORD GORING

Ah! I guessed as much!

SIR ROBERT CHILTERN (*looking at him*)

Really! How!

LORD GORING (*after some hesitation*)
Oh, merely by something in the expression of your face as you came in. Who told her?

SIR ROBERT CHILTERN
Mrs Cheveley herself. And the woman I love knows that I began my career with an act of low dishonesty, that I built up my life upon sands of shame – that I sold, like a common huckster, the secret that had been entrusted to me as a man of honour. I thank heaven poor Lord Radley died without knowing that I betrayed him. I would to God I had died before I had been so horribly tempted, or had fallen so low. (*burying his face in his hands*)

LORD GORING (*after a pause*)
You have heard nothing from Vienna yet, in answer to your wire?

SIR ROBERT CHILTERN (*looking up*)
Yes; I got a telegram from the first secretary at eight o'clock tonight.

LORD GORING
Well?

SIR ROBERT CHILTERN
Nothing is absolutely known against her. On the contrary, she occupies a rather high position in society. It is a sort of open secret that Baron Arnheim left her the greater portion of his immense fortune. Beyond that I can learn nothing.

LORD GORING
She doesn't turn out to be a spy, then?

SIR ROBERT CHILTERN
Oh! spies are of no use nowadays. Their profession is over. The newspapers do their work instead.

LORD GORING
And thunderingly well they do it.

SIR ROBERT CHILTERN
Arthur, I am parched with thirst. May I ring for something? Some hock and seltzer?

LORD GORING
Certainly. Let me. (*rings the bell*)

SIR ROBERT CHILTERN
Thanks! I don't know what to do, Arthur, I don't know what to do, and you are my only friend. But what a friend you are – the one friend I can trust. I can trust you absolutely, can't I?

LORD GORING
My dear Robert, of course. (*To* PHIPPS)
Bring some hock and seltzer.

PHIPPS
Yes, my lord.

LORD GORING
And Phipps!

PHIPPS
Yes, my lord.

LORD GORING

Will you excuse me for a moment, Robert? I
want to give some directions to my servant.

SIR ROBERT CHILTERN

Certainly.

LORD GORING

When that lady calls, tell her that I am not
expected home this evening. Tell her that I have
been suddenly called out of town. You understand?

PHIPPS

The lady is in that room, my lord. You told me
to show her into that room, my lord.

LORD GORING

You did perfectly right. (*exit* PHIPPS) What a mess
I am in. No; I think I shall get through it. I'll
give her a lecture through the door. Awkward
thing to manage, though.

SIR ROBERT CHILTERN

Arthur, tell me what I should do. My life seems
to have crumbled about me. I am a ship without
a rudder in a night without a star.

LORD GORING

Robert, you love your wife, don't you?

SIR ROBERT CHILTERN

I love her more than anything in the world. I
used to think ambition the great thing. It is not.

Love is the great thing in the world. There is nothing but love, and I love her. But I am defamed in her eyes. I am ignoble in her eyes. There is a wide gulf between us now. She has found me out, Arthur, she has found me out.

LORD GORING

Has she never in her life done some folly – some indiscretion – that she should not forgive your sin?

SIR ROBERT CHILTERN

My wife! Never! She does not know what weakness or temptation is. I am of clay like other men. She stands apart as good women do – pitiless in her perfection – cold and stern and without mercy. But I love her, Arthur. We are childless, and I have no one else to love, no one else to love me. Perhaps if God had sent us children she might have been kinder to me. But God has given us a lonely house. And she has cut my heart in two. Don't let us talk of it. I was brutal to her this evening. But I suppose when sinners talk to saints they are brutal always. I said to her things that were hideously true, on my side, from my standpoint, from the standpoint of men. But don't let us talk of that.

LORD GORING

Your wife will forgive you. Perhaps at this moment she is forgiving you. She loves you, Robert. Why should she not forgive?

SIR ROBERT CHILTERN

God grant it! God grant it! (*buries his face in his hands*) But there is something more I have to tell you, Arthur.

Enter PHIPPS *with drinks*

PHIPPS (*hands hock and seltzer to* SIR ROBERT CHILTERN)

Hock and seltzer, sir.

SIR ROBERT CHILTERN

Thank you.

LORD GORING

Is your carriage here, Robert?

SIR ROBERT CHILTERN

No, I walked from the club.

LORD GORING

Sir Robert will take my cab, Phipps.

PHIPPS

Yes, my lord.   (*exit*)

LORD GORING

Robert, you don't mind my sending you away?

SIR ROBERT CHILTERN

Arthur, you must let me stay for five minutes. I have made up my mind what I am going to do tonight in the House. The debate on the Argentine canal is to begin at eleven. (*A chair falls in the drawing-room*) What is that?

LORD GORING
  Nothing.

SIR ROBERT CHILTERN
  I heard a chair fall in the next room. Someone
  has been listening.

LORD GORING
  No, no; there is no one there.

SIR ROBERT CHILTERN
  There is someone. There are lights in the room,
  and the door is ajar. Someone has been listening
  to every secret of my life. Arthur, what does this
  mean?

LORD GORING
  Robert, you are excited, unnerved. I tell you
  there is no one in that room. Sit down, Robert.

SIR ROBERT CHILTERN
  Do you give me your word that there is no one
  there?

LORD GORING
  Yes.

SIR ROBERT CHILTERN
  Your word of honour? (*sits down*)

LORD GORING
  Yes.

SIR ROBERT CHILTERN (*rises*)
  Arthur, let me see for myself.

LORD GORING
  No, no.

SIR ROBERT CHILTERN
  If there is no one there why should I not look
  in that room? Arthur, you must let me go into
  that room and satisfy myself. Let me know that
  no eavesdropper has heard my life's secret.
  Arthur, you don't realise what I am going
  through.

LORD GORING
  Robert, this must stop. I have told you that there
  is no one in that room – that is enough.

SIR ROBERT CHILTERN (*rushes to the door of the room*)
  It is not enough. I insist on going into this room.
  You have told me there is no one there, so what
  reason can you have for refusing me?

LORD GORING
  For God's sake, don't! There is someone there.
  Someone whom you must not see.

SIR ROBERT CHILTERN
  Ah, I thought so!

LORD GORING
  I forbid you to enter that room.

SIR ROBERT CHILTERN
  Stand back. My life is at stake. And I don't care
  who is there. I will know who it is to whom I
  have told my secret and my shame. (*enters room*)

LORD GORING

Great heavens! his own wife!

SIR ROBERT CHILTERN *comes back, with a look of scorn and anger on his face*

SIR ROBERT CHILTERN

What explanation have you to give for the presence of that woman here?

LORD GORING

Robert, I swear to you on my honour that that lady is stainless and guiltless of all offence towards you.

SIR ROBERT CHILTERN

She is a vile, an infamous thing!

LORD GORING

Don't say that, Robert! It was for your sake she came here. It was to try and save you she came here. She loves you and no one else.

SIR ROBERT CHILTERN

You are mad. What have I to do with her intrigues with you? Let her remain your mistress! You are well suited to each other. She, corrupt and shameful – you, false as a friend, treacherous as an enemy even –

LORD GORING

It is not true, Robert. Before heaven, it is not true. In her presence and in yours I will explain all.

SIR ROBERT CHILTERN
  Let me pass, sir. You have lied enough upon your word of honour.

  > SIR ROBERT CHILTERN *goes out*. LORD GORING *rushes to the door of the drawing-room, when* MRS CHEVELEY *comes out, looking radiant and much amused*

MRS CHEVELEY (*with a mock curtsey*)
  Good-evening, Lord Goring!

LORD GORING
  Mrs Cheveley! Great heavens! . . . May I ask what you were doing in my drawing-room?

MRS CHEVELEY
  Merely listening. I have a perfect passion for listening through keyholes. One always hears such wonderful things through them.

LORD GORING
  Doesn't that sound rather like tempting Providence?

MRS CHEVELEY
  Oh! surely Providence can resist temptation by this time. (*makes a sign to him to take her cloak off, which he does*)

LORD GORING
  I am glad you have called. I am going to give you some good advice.

MRS CHEVELEY

Oh! pray don't. One should never give a woman anything that she can't wear in the evening.

LORD GORING

I see you are quite as wilful as you used to be.

MRS CHEVELEY

Far more! I have greatly improved. I have had more experience.

LORD GORING

Too much experience is a dangerous thing. Pray have a cigarette. Half the pretty women in London smoke cigarettes. Personally I prefer the other half.

MRS CHEVELEY

Thanks. I never smoke. My dressmaker wouldn't like it, and a woman's first duty in life is to her dressmaker, isn't it? What the second duty is, no one has as yet discovered.

LORD GORING

You have come here to sell me Robert Chiltern's letter, haven't you?

MRS CHEVELEY

To offer it to you on conditions! How did you guess that?

LORD GORING

Because you haven't mentioned the subject. Have you got it with you?

MRS CHEVELEY (*sitting down*)
  Oh, no! A well-made dress has no pockets.

LORD GORING
  What is your price for it?

MRS CHEVELEY
  How absurdly English you are! The English think
  that a cheque-book can solve every problem in
  life. Why, my dear Arthur, I have very much
  more money than you have, and quite as much
  as Robert Chiltern has got hold of. Money is
  not what I want.

LORD GORING
  What do you want then, Mrs Cheveley?

MRS CHEVELEY
  Why don't you call me Laura?

LORD GORING
  I don't like the name.

MRS CHEVELEY
  You used to adore it.

LORD GORING
  Yes; that's why. (MRS CHEVELEY *motions to him to
  sit down beside her. He smiles, and does so*)

MRS CHEVELEY
  Arthur, you loved me once.

LORD GORING
  Yes.

MRS CHEVELEY

And you asked me to be your wife.

LORD GORING

That was the natural result of my loving you.

MRS CHEVELEY

And you threw me over because you saw, or said you saw, poor old Lord Mortlake trying to have a violent flirtation with me in the conservatory at Tenby.

LORD GORING

I am under the impression that my lawyer settled that matter with you on certain terms . . . dictated by yourself.

MRS CHEVELEY

At that time I was poor; you were rich.

LORD GORING

Quite so. That is why you pretended to love me.

MRS CHEVELEY (*shrugging her shoulders*)

Poor old Lord Mortlake, who had only two topics of conversation, his gout and his wife! I never could quite make out which of the two he was talking about. He used the most horrible language about them both. Well, you were silly, Arthur. Why, Lord Mortlake was never anything more to me than an amusement. One of those utterly tedious amusements one only finds at an English country house on an English country Sunday. I don't think anyone at all morally responsible for what he or she does at an English country house.

LORD GORING
Yes, I know lots of people think that.

MRS CHEVELEY
I loved you, Arthur.

LORD GORING
My dear Mrs Cheveley, you have always been far too clever to know anything about love.

MRS CHEVELEY
I did love you. And you loved me. You know you loved me; and love is a very wonderful thing. I suppose that when a man has once loved a woman, he will do anything for her, except continue to love her? (*puts her hand on his*)

LORD GORING (*taking his hand away quietly*)
Yes; except that.

MRS CHEVELEY (*after a pause*)
I am tired of living abroad. I want to come back to London. I want to have a charming house here. I want to have a salon. If one could only teach the English how to talk, and the Irish how to listen, society here would be quite civilised. Besides, I have arrived at the romantic stage. When I saw you last night at the Chilterns, I knew you were the only person I had ever cared for, if I ever have cared for anybody, Arthur. And so, on the morning of the day you marry me, I

will give you Robert Chiltern's letter. That is my offer. I will give it to you now, if you promise to marry me.

LORD GORING
Now?

MRS CHEVELEY (*smiling*)
Tomorrow.

LORD GORING
Are you really serious?

MRS CHEVELEY
Yes, quite serious.

LORD GORING
I should make you a very bad husband.

MRS CHEVELEY
I don't mind bad husbands. I have had two. They amused me immensely.

LORD GORING
You mean that you amused yourself immensely, don't you?

MRS CHEVELEY
What do you know about my married life?

LORD GORING
Nothing; but I can read it like a book.

MRS CHEVELEY
What book?

LORD GORING (*rising*)

The Book of Numbers.

MRS CHEVELEY

Do you think it is quite charming of you to be so rude to a woman in your own house?

LORD GORING

In the case of very fascinating women, sex is a challenge, not a defence.

MRS CHEVELEY

I suppose that is meant for a compliment. My dear Arthur, women are never disarmed by compliments. Men always are. That is the difference between the two sexes.

LORD GORING

Women are never disarmed by anything, as far as I know them.

MRS CHEVELEY (*after a pause*)

Then you are going to allow your greatest friend, Robert Chiltern, to be ruined, rather than marry someone who really has considerable attractions left. I thought you would have risen to some great height of self-sacrifice, Arthur. I think you should. And the rest of your life you could spend in contemplating your own perfections.

LORD GORING

Oh! I do that as it is. And self-sacrifice is a thing that should be put down by law. It is so demoralising to the people for whom one sacrifices oneself. They always go to the bad.

MRS CHEVELEY

As if anything could demoralise Robert Chiltern! You seem to forget that I know his real character.

LORD GORING

What you know about him is not his real character. It was an act of folly done in his youth, dishonourable, I admit, shameful, I admit, unworthy of him, I admit, and therefore . . . not his true character.

MRS CHEVELEY

How you men stand up for each other!

LORD GORING

How you women war against each other!

MRS CHEVELEY (*bitterly*)

I only war against one woman, against Gertrude Chiltern. I hate her. I hate her now more than ever.

LORD GORING

Because you have brought a real tragedy into her life, I suppose.

MRS CHEVELEY (*with a sneer*)

Oh, there is only one real tragedy in a woman's life. The fact that her past is always her lover, and her future invariably her husband.

LORD GORING

Lady Chiltern knows nothing of the kind of life to which you are alluding.

MRS CHEVELEY

A woman whose size in gloves is seven and three-quarters never knows much about anything. You know Gertrude has always worn seven and three-quarters? That is one of the reasons why there was never any moral sympathy between us . . . Well, Arthur, I suppose this romantic interview may be regarded as at an end. You admit it was romantic, don't you? For the privilege of being your wife I was ready to surrender a great prize, the climax of my diplomatic career. You decline. Very well. If Sir Robert doesn't uphold my Argentine scheme, I expose him. *Voilà tout.*

LORD GORING

You musn't do that. It would be vile, horrible, infamous.

MRS CHEVELEY (*shrugging her shoulders*)

Oh! don't use big words. They mean so little. It is a commercial transaction. That is all. There is no good mixing up sentimentality in it. I offered to sell Robert Chiltern a certain thing. If he won't pay me my price, he will have to pay the world a greater price. There is no more to be said. I must go. Goodbye. Won't you shake hands?

LORD GORING

With you? No. Your transaction with Robert Chiltern may pass as a loathsome commercial transaction of a loathsome commercial age; but you seem to have forgotten that you came here tonight to talk of love; you whose lips desecrate the word love, you to whom the thing is a book closely sealed, went this afternoon to the house of one of the most noble and gentle women in the world to degrade her husband in her eyes, to try and kill her love for him, to put poison in her heart, and bitterness in her life, to break her idol, and, it may be, spoil her soul. That I cannot forgive you. That was horrible. For that there can be no forgiveness.

MRS CHEVELEY

Arthur, you are unjust to me. Believe me, you are quite unjust to me. I didn't go to taunt Gertrude at all. I had no idea of doing anything of the kind when I entered. I called with Lady Markby simply to ask whether an ornament, a jewel, that I lost somewhere last night, had been found at the Chilterns'. If you don't believe me, you can ask Lady Markby. She will tell you it is true. The scene that occurred happened after Lady Markby had left, and was really forced on me by Gertrude's rudeness and sneers. I called, oh! – a little out of malice if you like – but really to ask if a diamond brooch of mine had been found. That was the origin of the whole thing.

LORD GORING
A diamond snake-brooch with a ruby?

MRS CHEVELEY
Yes. How do you know?

LORD GORING
Because it is found. In point of fact, I found it
myself, and stupidly forgot to tell the butler
anything about it as I was leaving. (*goes over to
the writing-table and pulls out the drawers*) It is in
this drawer. No, that one. This is the brooch,
isn't it? (*holds up the brooch*)

MRS CHEVELEY
Yes. I am so glad to get it back. It was . . . a
present.

LORD GORING
Won't you wear it?

MRS CHEVELEY
Certainly, if you pin it in. (LORD GORING *suddenly
clasps it on her arm*) Why do you put it on as
a bracelet? I never knew it could be worn as a
bracelet.

LORD GORING
Really?

MRS CHEVELEY (*holding out her handsome arm*)
No; but it looks very well on me as a bracelet,
doesn't it?

LORD GORING
Yes; much better than when I saw it last.

MRS CHEVELEY
When did you see it last?

LORD GORING (*calmly*)
Oh, ten years ago, on Lady Berkshire, from whom you stole it.

MRS CHEVELEY (*starting*)
What do you mean?

LORD GORING
I mean that you stole that ornament from my cousin, Mary Berkshire, to whom I gave it when she was married. Suspicion fell on a wretched servant, who was sent away in disgrace. I recognised it last night. I determined to say nothing about it till I had found the thief. I have found the thief now, and I have heard her own confession.

MRS CHEVELEY (*tossing her head*)
It is not true.

LORD GORING
You know it is true. Why, thief is written across your face at this moment.

MRS CHEVELEY
I will deny the whole affair from beginning to end. I will say that I have never seen this wretched thing, that it was never in my possession.

MRS CHEVELEY *tries to get the bracelet off her arm, but fails.* LORD GORING *looks on amused. Her thin fingers tear at the jewel to no purpose. A curse breaks from her*

LORD GORING

The drawback of stealing a thing, Mrs Cheveley, is that one never knows how wonderful the thing that one steals is. You can't get that bracelet off, unless you know where the spring is. And I see you don't know where the spring is. It is rather difficult to find.

MRS CHEVELEY

You brute! You coward! (*she tries again to unclasp the bracelet, but fails*)

LORD GORING

Oh! don't use big words. They mean so little.

MRS CHEVELEY (*again tears at the bracelet in a paroxysm of rage, with inarticulate sounds. Then stops, and looks at* LORD GORING)

What are you going to do?

LORD GORING

I am going to ring for my servant. He is an admirable servant. Always comes in the moment one rings for him. When he comes I will tell him to fetch the police.

MRS CHEVELEY (*trembling*)

The police? What for?

144

LORD GORING

Tomorrow the Berkshires will prosecute you.
That is what the police are for.

MRS CHEVELEY (*is now in an agony of physical terror.
Her face is distorted. Her mouth awry. A mask has
fallen from her. She is, for the moment, dreadful to
look at*)
Don't do that. I will do anything you want.
Anything in the world you want.

LORD GORING

Give me Robert Chiltern's letter.

MRS CHEVELEY

Stop! Stop! Let me have time to think.

LORD GORING

Give me Robert Chiltern's letter.

MRS CHEVELEY

I have not got it with me. I will give it to you
tomorrow.

LORD GORING

You know you are lying. Give it to me at once.
(MRS CHEVELEY *pulls the letter out, and hands it to
him. She is horribly pale*) This is it?

MRS CHEVELEY (*in a hoarse voice*)
Yes.

LORD GORING (*takes the letter, examines it, sighs, and
burns it over the lamp*)
For so well-dressed a woman, Mrs Cheveley, you

have moments of admirable common sense. I congratulate you.

MRS CHEVELEY (*catches sight of* LADY CHILTERN'S *letter, the cover of which is just showing from under the blotting-book*)
Please get me a glass of water.

LORD GORING
Certainly. (*Goes to the corner of the room and pours out a glass of water. While his back is turned* MRS CHEVELEY *steals* LADY CHILTERN'S *letter. When* LORD GORING *returns with the glass she refuses it with a gesture*)

MRS CHEVELEY
Thank you. Will you help me on with my cloak?

LORD GORING
With pleasure. (*puts her cloak on*)

MRS CHEVELEY
Thanks. I am never going to try to harm Robert Chiltern again.

LORD GORING
Fortunately you have not the chance, Mrs Cheveley.

MRS CHEVELEY
Well, if even I had the chance, I wouldn't. On the contrary, I am going to render him a great service.

LORD GORING
I am charmed to hear it. It is a reformation.

MRS CHEVELEY

Yes. I can't bear so upright a gentleman, so honourable an English gentleman, being so shamefully deceived and so –

LORD GORING

Well?

MRS CHEVELEY

I find that somehow Gertrude Chiltern's dying speech and confession has strayed into my pocket.

LORD GORING

What do you mean?

MRS CHEVELEY (*with a bitter note of triumph in her voice*)

I mean that I am going to send Robert Chiltern the love-letter his wife wrote to you tonight.

LORD GORING

Love-letter?

MRS CHEVELEY (*laughing*)

'I want you. I trust you. I am coming to you. Gertrude.'

LORD GORING *rushes to the bureau and takes up the envelope, finds it empty, and turns round*

LORD GORING

You wretched woman, must you always be thieving? Give me back that letter. I'll take it from you by force. You shall not leave my room till I have got it.

147

He rushes towards her, but MRS CHEVELEY
*at once puts her hand on the electric bell that
is on the table. The bell sounds with shrill
reverberations, and* PHIPPS *enters*

MRS CHEVELEY (*after a pause*)
Lord Goring merely rang that you should show
me out. Good-night, Lord Goring!

Goes out followed by PHIPPS. *Her face is
illumined with evil triumph. There is joy in
her eyes. Youth seems to come back to her. Her
last glance is like a swift arrow.* LORD GORING
bites his lip, and lights a cigarette

END OF ACT THREE

ACT FOUR

Same as Act Two. LORD GORING *is standing by the fireplace with his hands in his pockets. He is looking rather bored.*

LORD GORING (*pulls out his watch, inspects it, and rings the bell*)
It is a great nuisance. I can't find anyone in this house to talk to. And I am full of interesting information. I feel like the latest edition of something or other.

Enter SERVANT

JAMES
Sir Robert is still at the Foreign Office, my lord.

LORD GORING
Lady Chiltern not down yet?

JAMES
Her ladyship has not yet left her room. Miss Chiltern has just come in from riding.

149

LORD GORING (*to himself*)
Ah! that is something.

JAMES
Lord Caversham has been waiting some time in the library for Sir Robert. I told him your lordship was here.

LORD GORING
Thank you. Would you kindly tell him I've gone?

JAMES (*bowing*)
I shall do so, my lord.

Exit SERVANT

LORD GORING
Really, I don't want to meet my father three days running. It is a great deal too much excitement for any son. I hope to goodness he won't come up. Fathers should be neither seen nor heard. That is the only proper basis for family life. Mothers are different. Mothers are darlings. (*throws himself down into a chair, picks up a paper and begins to read it*)

Enter LORD CAVERSHAM

LORD CAVERSHAM
Well, sir, what are you doing here? Wasting your time as usual, I suppose?

LORD GORING (*throws down paper and rises*)
My dear father, when one pays a visit it is for

the purpose of wasting other people's time, not one's own.

LORD CAVERSHAM
Have you been thinking over what I spoke to you about last night?

LORD GORING
I have been thinking about nothing else.

LORD CAVERSHAM
Engaged to be married yet?

LORD GORING (*genially*)
Not yet; but I hope to be before lunchtime.

LORD CAVERSHAM (*caustically*)
You can have till dinnertime if it would be of any convenience to you.

LORD GORING
Thanks awfully, but I think I'd sooner be engaged before lunch.

LORD CAVERSHAM
Humph! Never know when you are serious or not.

LORD GORING
Neither do I, father.

A pause

LORD CAVERSHAM
I suppose you have read *The Times* this morning?

LORD GORING (*airily*)

The Times? Certainly not. I only read the *Morning Post.* All that one should know about modern life is where the duchesses are; anything else is quite demoralising.

LORD CAVERSHAM

Do you mean to say you have not read *The Times* leading article on Robert Chiltern's career?

LORD GORING

Good heavens! No. What does it say?

LORD CAVERSHAM

What should it say, sir? Everything complimentary, of course. Chiltern's speech last night on this Argentine Canal Scheme was one of the finest pieces of oratory ever delivered in the House since Canning.

LORD GORING

Ah! Never heard of Canning. Never wanted to. And did . . . did Chiltern uphold the scheme?

LORD CAVERSHAM

Uphold it, sir? How little you know him! Why, he denounced it roundly, and the whole system of modern political finance. This speech is the turning-point in his career, as *The Times* points out. You should read this article, sir. (*Opens* The Times) 'Sir Robert Chiltern . . . most rising of our young statesmen . . . Brilliant orator . . . Unblemished career . . . Well-known integrity of character . . . Represents what is best in English public life . . . Noble contrast to the lax morality so common among foreign politicians.' They will never say that of you, sir.

LORD GORING

I sincerely hope not, father. However, I am delighted at what you tell me about Robert, thoroughly delighted. It shows he has got pluck.

LORD CAVERSHAM

He has got more than pluck, sir, he has got genius.

LORD GORING

Ah! I prefer pluck. It is not so common, nowadays, as genius is.

LORD CAVERSHAM

I wish you would go into Parliament.

LORD GORING

My dear father, only people who look dull ever get into the House of Commons, and only people who are dull ever succeed there.

LORD CAVERSHAM

Why don't you try to do something useful in life?

LORD GORING

I am far too young.

LORD CAVERSHAM (*testily*)

I hate this affectation of youth, sir. It is a great deal too prevalent nowadays.

LORD GORING
Youth isn't an affectation. Youth is an art.

LORD CAVERSHAM
Why don't you propose to that pretty Miss Chiltern?

LORD GORING
I am of a very nervous disposition, especially in the morning.

LORD CAVERSHAM
I don't suppose there is the smallest chance of her accepting you.

LORD GORING
I don't know how the betting stands today.

LORD CAVERSHAM
If she did accept you she would be the prettiest fool in England.

LORD GORING
That is just what I should like to marry. A thoroughly sensible wife would reduce me to a condition of absolute idiocy in less than six months.

LORD CAVERSHAM
You don't deserve her, sir.

LORD GORING
My dear father, if we men married the women we deserved, we should have a very bad time of it.

Enter MABEL CHILTERN

MABEL CHILTERN

Oh! . . . How do you do, Lord Caversham? I hope Lady Caversham is quite well?

LORD CAVERSHAM

Lady Caversham is as usual, as usual.

LORD GORING

Good-morning, Miss Mabel!

MABEL CHILTERN (*taking no notice at all of* LORD GORING, *and addressing herself exclusively to* LORD CAVERSHAM)

And Lady Caversham's bonnets . . . are they at all better?

LORD CAVERSHAM

They have had a serious relapse, I am sorry to say.

LORD GORING

Good-morning, Miss Mabel.

MABEL CHILTERN (*to* LORD CAVERSHAM)

I hope an operation will not be necessary.

LORD CAVERSHAM (*smiling at her pertness*)

If it is, we shall have to give Lady Caversham a narcotic. Otherwise she would never consent to have a feather touched.

LORD GORING (*with increased emphasis*)

Good-morning, Miss Mabel!

MABEL CHILTERN (*turning round with feigned surprise*)

Oh, are you here? Of course you understand that

after your breaking your appointment I am never going to speak to you again.

LORD GORING

Oh, please don't say such a thing. You are the one person in London I really like to have to listen to me.

MABEL CHILTERN

Lord Goring, I never believe a single word that either you or I say to each other.

LORD CAVERSHAM

You are quite right, my dear, quite right as far as he is concerned, I mean.

MABEL CHILTERN

Do you think you could possibly make your son behave a little better occasionally? Just as a change.

LORD CAVERSHAM

I regret to say, Miss Chiltern, that I have no influence at all over my son. I wish I had. If I had, I know what I would make him do.

MABEL CHILTERN

I am afraid that he has one of those terribly weak natures that are not susceptible to influence.

LORD CAVERSHAM

He is very heartless, very heartless.

LORD GORING

It seems to me that I am a little in the way here.

MABEL CHILTERN

It is very good for you to be in the way, and to know what people say of you behind your back.

LORD GORING

I don't at all like knowing what people say of me behind my back. It makes me far too conceited.

LORD CAVERSHAM

After that, my dear, I really must bid you good-morning.

MABEL CHILTERN

Oh! I hope you are not going to leave me all alone with Lord Goring? Especially at such an early hour in the day.

LORD CAVERSHAM

I am afraid I can't take him with me to Downing Street. It is not the Prime Minister's day for seeing the unemployed.

Shakes hands with MABEL CHILTERN, *takes up his hat and stick, and goes out, with a parting glare of indignation at* LORD GORING

MABEL CHILTERN (*takes up roses and begins to arrange them in a bowl on the table*)

People who don't keep their appointments in the park are horrid.

LORD GORING

Detestable.

MABEL CHILTERN

I am glad you admit it. But I wish you wouldn't look so pleased about it.

LORD GORING

I can't help it. I always look pleased when I am with you.

MABEL CHILTERN (*sadly*)

Then I suppose it is my duty to remain with you?

LORD GORING

Of course it is.

MABEL CHILTERN

Well, my duty is a thing I never do, on principle. It always depresses me. So I am afraid I must leave you.

LORD GORING

Please don't, Miss Mabel. I have something very particular to say to you.

MABEL CHILTERN (*rapturously*)

Oh! is it a proposal?

LORD GORING (*somewhat taken aback*)

Well, yes, it is – I am bound to say it is.

MABEL CHILTERN (*with a sigh of pleasure*)

I am so glad. That makes the second today.

LORD GORING (*indignantly*)

The second today? What conceited ass has been impertinent enough to dare to propose to you before I proposed to you?

MABEL CHILTERN

Tommy Trafford, of course. It is one of Tommy's days for proposing. He always proposes on Tuesdays and Thursdays, during the season.

LORD GORING

You didn't accept him, I hope?

MABEL CHILTERN

I make it a rule never to accept Tommy. That is why he goes on proposing. Of course, as you didn't turn up this morning, I very nearly said yes. It would have been an excellent lesson both for him and for you if I had. It would have taught you both better manners.

LORD GORING

Oh! bother Tommy Trafford. Tommy is a silly little ass. I love you.

MABEL CHILTERN

I know. And I think you might have mentioned it before. I am sure I have given you heaps of opportunities.

LORD GORING

Mabel, do be serious. Please be serious.

MABEL CHILTERN

Ah! that is the sort of thing a man always says to a girl before he has been married to her. He never says it afterwards.

LORD GORING (*taking hold of her hand*)
Mabel, I have told you that I love you. Can't you love me a little in return?

MABEL CHILTERN
You silly Arthur! If you knew anything about . . . anything, which you don't, you would know that I adore you. Everyone in London knows it except you. It is a public scandal the way I adore you. I have been going about for the last six months telling the whole of society that I adore you. I wonder you consent to have anything to say to me. I have no character left at all. At least, I feel so happy that I am quite sure I have no character left at all.

LORD GORING (*catches her in his arms and kisses her. Then there is a pause of bliss*)
Dear! Do you know I was awfully afraid of being refused!

MABEL CHILTERN (*looking up at him*)
But you never have been refused yet by anybody, have you, Arthur? I can't imagine anyone refusing you.

LORD GORING (*after kissing her again*)
Of course I'm not nearly good enough for you, Mabel.

MABEL CHILTERN (*nestling close to him*)
I am so glad, darling. I was afraid you were.

LORD GORING (*after some hesitation*)
And I'm . . . I'm a little over thirty.

MABEL CHILTERN
Dear, you look weeks younger than that.

LORD GORING (*enthusiastically*)
How sweet of you to say so! . . . And it is only
fair to tell you frankly that I am fearfully extra-
vagant.

MABEL CHILTERN
But so am I, Arthur. So we're sure to agree. And
now I must go and see Gertrude.

LORD GORING
Must you really? (*kisses her*)

MABEL CHILTERN
Yes.

LORD GORING
Then do tell her I want to talk to her particularly.
I have been waiting here all the morning to see
either her or Robert.

MABEL CHILTERN
Do you mean to say you didn't come here
expressly to propose to me?

LORD GORING (*triumphantly*)
No; that was a flash of genius.

MABEL CHILTERN
Your first.

LORD GORING (*with determination*)
My last.

MABEL CHILTERN
I am delighted to hear it. Now don't stir. I'll be back in five minutes. And don't fall into any temptations while I am away.

LORD GORING
Dear Mabel, while you are away, there are none. It makes me horribly dependent on you.

Enter LADY CHILTERN

LADY CHILTERN
Good-morning, dear! How pretty you are looking!

MABEL CHILTERN
How pale you are looking, Gertrude! It is most becoming!

LADY CHILTERN
Good-morning, Lord Goring!

LORD GORING (*bowing*)
Good-morning, Lady Chiltern!

MABEL CHILTERN (*aside to* LORD GORING)
I shall be in the conservatory, under the second palm tree on the left.

LORD GORING
Second on the left?

MABEL CHILTERN (*with a look of mock surprise*)
Yes; the usual palm tree.

Blows a kiss to him, unobserved by LADY CHILTERN, *and goes out*

LORD GORING
Lady Chiltern, I have a certain amount of very good news to tell you. Mrs Cheveley gave me up Robert's letter last night, and I burned it. Robert is safe.

LADY CHILTERN (*sinking on the sofa*)
Safe! Oh! I am so glad of that. What a good friend you are to him – to us!

LORD GORING
There is only one person now that could be said to be in any danger.

LADY CHILTERN
Who is that?

LORD GORING (*sitting down beside her*)
Yourself.

LADY CHILTERN
I! In danger? What do you mean?

LORD GORING
Danger is too great a word. It is a word I should not have used. But I admit I have something to tell you that may distress you, that terribly distresses me. Yesterday evening you wrote me a very beautiful, womanly letter, asking me for my help. You wrote to me as one of your oldest friends, one of your husband's

oldest friends. Mrs Cheveley stole that letter from my rooms.

LADY CHILTERN
Well, what use is it to her? Why should she not have it?

LORD GORING (*rising*)
Lady Chiltern, I will be quite frank with you. Mrs Cheveley puts a certain construction on that letter and proposes to send it to your husband.

LADY CHILTERN
But what construction could she put on it? . . . Oh! not that! not that! If I in – in trouble, and wanting your help, trusting you, propose to come to you . . . that you may advise me . . . assist me . . . Oh! are there women so horrible as that . . . ? And she proposes to send it to my husband? Tell me what happened. Tell me all that happened.

LORD GORING
Mrs Cheveley was concealed in a room adjoining my library, without my knowledge. I thought that the person who was waiting in that room to see me was yourself. Robert came in unexpectedly. A chair or something fell in the room. He forced his way in, and he discovered her. We had a terrible scene. I still thought it was you. He left me in anger. At the end of everything Mrs Cheveley got possession of your letter – she stole it, when or how, I don't know.

LADY CHILTERN

At what hour did this happen?

LORD GORING

At half-past ten. And now I propose that we tell Robert the whole thing at once.

LADY CHILTERN (*looking at him with amazement that is almost terror*)

You want me to tell Robert that the woman you expected was not Mrs Cheveley, but myself? That it was I whom you thought was concealed in a room in your house, at half-past ten o'clock at night? You want me to tell him that?

LORD GORING

I think it is better that he should know the exact truth.

LADY CHILTERN (*rising*)

Oh, I couldn't, I couldn't!

LORD GORING

May I do it?

LADY CHILTERN

No.

LORD GORING (*gravely*)

You are wrong, Lady Chiltern.

LADY CHILTERN

No. The letter must be intercepted. That is all. But how can I do it? Letters arrive for him every moment of the day. His secretaries open them and hand them to him. I dare not ask the servants to bring me his letters. It would be impossible. Oh! why don't you tell me what to do?

LORD GORING
Pray be calm, Lady Chiltern, and answer the questions I am going to put to you. You said his secretaries open his letters.

LADY CHILTERN
Yes.

LORD GORING
Who is with him today? Mr Trafford, isn't it?

LADY CHILTERN
No. Mr Montford, I think.

LORD GORING
You can trust him?

LADY CHILTERN (*with a gesture of despair*)
Oh! how do I know?

LORD GORING
He would do what you asked him, wouldn't he?

LADY CHILTERN
I think so.

LORD GORING
Your letter was on pink paper. He could recognise it without reading it, couldn't he? By the colour?

LADY CHILTERN
I suppose so.

LORD GORING
Is he in the house now?

LADY CHILTERN
Yes.

LORD GORING
Then I will go and see him myself, and tell him that a certain letter, written on pink paper, is to be forwarded to Robert today, and that at all costs it must not reach him. (*goes to the door, and opens it*) Oh! Robert is coming upstairs with the letter in his hand. It has reached him already.

LADY CHILTERN (*with a cry of pain*)
Oh! you have saved his life; what have you done with mine?

> *Enter* SIR ROBERT CHILTERN. *He has the letter in his hand, and is reading it. He comes towards his wife, not noticing* LORD GORING's *presence*

SIR ROBERT CHILTERN
'I want you. I trust you. I am coming to you. Gertrude.' Oh, my love! Is this true? Do you indeed trust me, and want me? If so, it was for me to come to you, not for you to write of coming to me. This letter of yours, Gertrude, makes me feel that nothing that the world may do can hurt me now. You want me, Gertrude.

LORD GORING, *unseen by* SIR ROBERT CHILTERN, *makes an imploring sign to* LADY CHILTERN to *accept the situation and* SIR ROBERT CHILTERN'S *error.*

LADY CHILTERN
Yes.

SIR ROBERT CHILTERN
You trust me, Gertrude?

LADY CHILTERN
Yes.

SIR ROBERT CHILTERN
Ah! why did you not add you loved me?

LADY CHILTERN (*taking his hand*)
Because I loved you.

LORD GORING *passes into the conservatory*

SIR ROBERT CHILTERN (*kisses her*)
Gertrude, you don't know what I feel. When Montford passed me your letter across the table – he had opened it by mistake, I suppose, without looking at the handwriting on the envelope – and I read it – oh! I did not care what disgrace or punishment was in store for me, I only thought you loved me still.

LADY CHILTERN
There is no disgrace in store for you, nor any public shame. Mrs Cheveley has handed over to

Lord Goring the document that was in her possession, and he has destroyed it.

SIR ROBERT CHILTERN
Are you sure of this, Gertrude?

LADY CHILTERN
Yes; Lord Goring has just told me.

SIR ROBERT CHILTERN
Then I am safe! Oh! what a wonderful thing to be safe! For two days I have been in terror. I am safe now. How did Arthur destroy my letter? Tell me.

LADY CHILTERN
He burned it.

SIR ROBERT CHILTERN
I wish I had seen that one sin of my youth burning to ashes. How many men there are in modern life who would like to see their past burning to white ashes before them! Is Arthur still here?

LADY CHILTERN
Yes; he is in the conservatory.

SIR ROBERT CHILTERN
I am so glad now I made that speech last night in the House, so glad. I made it thinking that public disgrace might be the result. But it has not been so.

LADY CHILTERN
  Public honour has been the result.

SIR ROBERT CHILTERN
  I think so. I fear so, almost. For although I am
  safe from detection, although every proof against
  me is destroyed, I suppose, Gertrude . . . I
  suppose I should retire from public life? (*he looks
  anxiously at his wife*)

LADY CHILTERN (*eagerly*)
  Oh yes, Robert, you should do that. It is your
  duty to do that.

SIR ROBERT CHILTERN
  It is much to surrender.

LADY CHILTERN
  No; it will be much to gain.

  SIR ROBERT CHILTERN *walks up and down the
  room with a troubled expression. Then comes
  over to his wife, and puts his hand on her
  shoulder*

SIR ROBERT CHILTERN
  And you would be happy living somewhere alone
  with me, abroad perhaps, or in the country away
  from London, away from public life? You would
  have no regrets?

LADY CHILTERN
  Oh! none, Robert.

SIR ROBERT CHILTERN (*sadly*)

And your ambition for me? You used to be ambitious for me.

LADY CHILTERN

Oh, my ambition! I have none now, but that we two may love each other. It was your ambition that led you astray. Let us not talk about ambition.

LORD GORING returns from the conservatory, looking very pleased with himself, and with an entirely new buttonhole that someone has made for him

SIR ROBERT CHILTERN (*going towards him*)

Arthur, I have to thank you for what you have done for me. I don't know how I can repay you. (*shakes hands with him*)

LORD GORING

My dear fellow, I'll tell you at once. At the present moment, under the usual palm tree . . . I mean in the conservatory . . .

Enter MASON

MASON

Lord Caversham.

LORD GORING

That admirable father of mine really makes a habbit of turning up at the wrong moment. It is very heartless of him, very heartless indeed.

Enter LORD CAVERSHAM. MASON *goes out*

171

LORD CAVERSHAM

Good-morning, Lady Chiltern! Warmest congrat-
ulations to you, Chiltern, on your brilliant speech
last night. I have just left the Prime Minister,
and you are to have the vacant seat in the cabinet.

SIR ROBERT CHILTERN (*with a look of joy and triumph*)
A seat in the cabinet?

LORD CAVERSHAM

Yes, here is the Prime Minister's letter. (*hands letter*)

SIR ROBERT CHILTERN (*takes letter and reads it*)
A seat in the cabinet!

LORD CAVERSHAM

Certainly, and you well deserve it too. You have
got what we want so much in political life nowadays – high character, high moral tone, high
principles. (*To* LORD GORING)
    Everything that you have not got, sir, and
never will have.

LORD GORING

I don't like principles, father. I prefer prejudices.

SIR ROBERT CHILTERN *is on the brink of*
accepting the Prime Minister's offer, when he
sees his wife looking at him with her clear,
candid eyes. He then realises that it is impossible

SIR ROBERT CHILTERN

I cannot accept this offer, Lord Caversham. I
have made up my mind to decline it.

LORD CAVERSHAM
Decline it, sir!

SIR ROBERT CHILTERN
My intention is to retire at once from public life.

LORD CAVERSHAM (*angrily*)
Decline a seat in the cabinet, and retire from public life? Never heard such damned nonsense in the whole course of my existence. I beg your pardon, Lady Chiltern. Chiltern, I beg your pardon. (*To* LORD GORING)
Don't grin like that, sir.

LORD GORING
No, father.

LORD CAVERSHAM
Lady Chiltern, you are a sensible woman, the most sensible woman in London, the most sensible woman I know. Will you kindly prevent your husband from making such a . . . from talking such . . . Will you kindly do that, Lady Chiltern?

LADY CHILTERN
I think my husband is right in his determination, Lord Caversham. I approve of it.

LORD CAVERSHAM
You approve of it? Good heavens!

LADY CHILTERN (*taking her husband's hand*)
I admire him for it. I admire him immensely for it. I have never admired him so much before.

He is finer than even I thought him. (*To* SIR ROBERT CHILTERN)

You will go and write your letter to the Prime Minister now, won't you? Don't hesitate about it, Robert.

SIR ROBERT CHILTERN (*with a touch of bitterness*)
I suppose I had better write it at once. Such offers are not repeated. I will ask you to excuse me for a moment, Lord Caversham.

LADY CHILTERN
I may come with you, Robert, may I not?

SIR ROBERT CHILTERN
Yes, Gertrude.

LADY CHILTERN *goes with him*

LORD CAVERSHAM
What is the matter with this family? Something wrong here, eh? (*tapping his forehead*) Idiocy? Hereditary, I suppose. Both of them, too. Wife as well as husband. Very sad. Very sad indeed! And they are not an old family. Can't understand it.

LORD GORING
It is not idiocy, father, I assure you.

LORD CAVERSHAM
What is it then, sir?

LORD GORING (*after some hesitation*)
Well, it is what is called nowadays a high moral tone, father. That is all.

LORD CAVERSHAM

Hate these new-fangled names. Same thing as we used to call idiocy fifty years ago. Shan't stay in this house any longer.

LORD GORING (*taking his arm*)

Oh! just go in here for a moment, father. Third palm tree to the left, the usual palm tree.

LORD CAVERSHAM

What, sir?

LORD GORING

I beg your pardon, father, I forgot. The conservatory, father, the conservatory – there is someone there I want you to talk to.

LORD CAVERSHAM

What about, sir?

LORD GORING

About me, father.

LORD CAVERSHAM (*grimly*)

Not a subject on which much eloquence is possible.

LORD GORING

No, father; but the lady is like me. She doesn't care much for eloquence in others. She thinks it a little loud.

LORD CAVERSHAM *goes into the conservatory.*
LADY CHILTERN *enters*

LORD GORING

Lady Chiltern, why are you playing Mrs Cheveley's cards?

LADY CHILTERN (*startled*)

I don't understand you.

LORD GORING

Mrs Cheveley made an attempt to ruin your husband. Either to drive him from public life, or to make him adopt a dishonourable position. From the latter tragedy you saved him. The former you are now thrusting on him. Why should you do him the wrong Mrs Cheveley tried to do and failed?

LADY CHILTERN

Lord Goring?

LORD GORING (*pulling himself together for a great effort, and showing the philosopher that underlies the dandy*)

Lady Chiltern, allow me. You wrote me a letter last night in which you said you trusted me and wanted my help. Now is the moment when you really want my help, now is the time when you have got to trust me, to trust in my counsel and judgement. You love Robert. Do you want to kill his love for you? What sort of existence will he have if you rob him of the fruits of his ambition, if you take him from the splendour of a great political career, if you close the doors of public life against him, if you condemn him to sterile failure, he who was made for triumph and success? Women are not meant to judge us, but to forgive us when we need forgiveness. Pardon, not punishment, is their mission. Why should you scourge him with rods for a sin done in his youth, before he knew you, before he knew himself? A man's life is of more value than a woman's. It has larger issues, wider scope, greater ambitions. A woman's life revolves in curves of emotions. It is upon lines of intellect that a man's life progresses. Don't make any terrible mistake, Lady Chiltern. A woman who can keep a man's love, and love him in return, has done all the world wants of women, or should want of them.

LADY CHILTERN (*troubled and hesitating*)
But it is my husband himself who wishes to retire from public life. He feels it is his duty. It was he who first said so.

LORD GORING
Rather than lose your love, Robert would do anything, wreck his whole career, as he is on the brink of doing now. He is making for you a terrible sacrifice. Take my advice, Lady Chiltern, and do not accept a sacrifice so great. If you do, you will live to repent it bitterly. We men and women are not made to accept such sacrifices from each other. We are not worthy of them. Besides, Robert has been punished enough.

LADY CHILTERN

We have both been punished. I set him up too high.

LORD GORING (*with deep feeling in his voice*)

Do not for that reason set him down now too low. If he has fallen from his altar, do not thrust him into the mire. Failure to Robert would be the very mire of shame. Power is his passion. He would lose everything, even his power to feel love. Your husband's life is at this moment in your hands, your husband's love is in your hands. Don't mar both for him.

Enter SIR ROBERT CHILTERN

SIR ROBERT CHILTERN

Gertrude, here is the draft of my letter. Shall I read it to you?

LADY CHILTERN

Let me see it.

SIR ROBERT CHILTERN *hands her the letter. She reads it and then, with a gesture of passion, tears it up*

SIR ROBERT CHILTERN

What are you doing?

LADY CHILTERN

A man's life is of more value than a woman's. It has larger issues, wider scope, greater ambitions. Our lives revolve in curves of emotions. It is upon lines of intellect that a man's life progresses. I have just learnt this, and much else with it, from Lord Goring. And I will not spoil your life for you, nor see you spoil it as a sacrifice to me, a useless sacrifice!

SIR ROBERT CHILTERN
Gertrude! Gertrude!

LADY CHILTERN
You can forget. Men easily forget. And I forgive. That is how women help the world. I see that now.

SIR ROBERT CHILTERN (*deeply overcome by emotion, embraces her*)
My wife! my wife! (*To* LORD GORING)
Arthur, it seems that I am always to be in your debt.

LORD GORING
Oh dear no, Robert. Your debt is to Lady Chiltern, not to me!

SIR ROBERT CHILTERN
I owe you much. And now tell me what you were going to ask me just now as Lord Caversham came in.

LORD GORING
Robert, you are your sister's guardian, and I want your consent to my marriage with her. That is all.

LADY CHILTERN

Oh, I am so glad! I am so glad! (*Shakes hands with* LORD GORING)

LORD GORING

Thank you, Lady Chiltern.

SIR ROBERT CHILTERN (*with a troubled look*)

My sister to be your wife?

LORD GORING

Yes.

SIR ROBERT CHILTERN (*speaking with great firmness*)

Arthur, I am very sorry, but the thing is quite out of the question. I have to think of Mabel's future happiness. And I don't think her happiness would be safe in your hands. And I cannot have her sacrificed!

LORD GORING

Sacrificed!

SIR ROBERT CHILTERN

Yes, utterly sacrificed. Loveless marriages are horrible. But there is one thing worse than an absolutely loveless marriage. A marriage in which there is love, but on one side only; faith, but on one side only; devotion, but on one side only, and in which of the two hearts one is sure to be broken.

LORD GORING

But I love Mabel. No other woman has any place in my life.

LADY CHILTERN

Robert, if they love each other, why should they not be married?

SIR ROBERT CHILTERN

Arthur cannot bring Mabel the love that she deserves.

LORD GORING

What reason have you for saying that?

SIR ROBERT CHILTERN (*after a pause*)

Do you really require me to tell you?

LORD GORING

Certainly I do.

SIR ROBERT CHILTERN

As you choose. When I called on you yesterday evening I found Mrs Cheveley concealed in your rooms. It was between ten and eleven o'clock at night. I do not wish to say anything more. Your relations with Mrs Cheveley have, as I said to you last night, nothing whatsoever to do with me. I know you were engaged to be married to her once. The fascination she exercised over you then seems to have returned. You spoke to me last night of her as of a woman pure and stainless, a woman whom you respected and honoured. That may be so. But I cannot give my sister's life into your hands. It would be wrong of me. It would be unjust, infamously unjust to her.

LORD GORING

I have nothing more to say.

LADY CHILTERN

Robert, it was not Mrs Cheveley whom Lord Goring expected last night.

SIR ROBERT CHILTERN

Not Mrs Cheveley! Who was it then?

LORD GORING

Lady Chiltern.

LADY CHILTERN

It was your own wife. Robert, yesterday afternoon Lord Goring told me that if ever I was in trouble I could come to him for help, as he was our oldest and best friend. Later on, after that terrible scene in this room, I wrote to him telling him that I trusted him, that I had need of him, that I was coming to him for help and advice. (SIR ROBERT CHILTERN *takes the letter out of his pocket*) Yes, that letter. I didn't go to Lord Goring's, after all. I felt that it is from ourselves alone that help can come. Pride made me think that. Mrs Cheveley went. She stole my letter and sent it anonymously to you this morning, that you should think . . . Oh! Robert, I cannot tell you what she wished you to think . . .

SIR ROBERT CHILTERN

What! Had I fallen so low in your eyes that you

thought that even for a moment I could have doubted your goodness? Gertrude, Gertrude, you are to me the white image of all good things, and sin can never touch you. Arthur, you can go to Mabel, and you have my best wishes! Oh! stop a moment. There is no name at the beginning of this letter. The brilliant Mrs Cheveley does not seem to have noticed that. There should be a name.

LADY CHILTERN
Let me write yours. It is you I trust and need. You and none else.

LORD GORING
Well, really, Lady Chiltern, I think I should have back my own letter.

LADY CHILTERN (*smiling*)
No; you shall have Mabel. (*takes the letter and writes her husband's name on it*)

LORD GORING
Well, I hope she hasn't changed her mind. It's nearly twenty minutes since I saw her last.

Enter MABEL CHILTERN *and* LORD CAVERSHAM

MABEL CHILTERN
Lord Goring, I think your father's conversation much more improving than yours. I am only going to talk to Lord Caversham in the future, and always under the usual palm tree.

LORD GORING

Darling! (*kisses her*)

LORD CAVERSHAM (*considerably taken aback*)

What does this mean, sir? You don't mean to say that this charming, clever young lady has been so foolish as to accept you?

LORD GORING

Certainly, father! And Chiltern's been wise enough to accept the seat in the cabinet.

LORD CAVERSHAM

I am very glad to hear that, Chiltern . . . I congratulate you, sir. If the country doesn't go to the dogs or the Radicals, we shall have you prime minister, someday.

Enter MASON

MASON

Luncheon is on the table, my lady! (MASON *goes out*)

MABEL CHILTERN

You'll stop to luncheon, Lord Caversham, won't you?

LORD CAVERSHAM

With pleasure, and I'll drive you down to Downing Street afterwards, Chiltern. You have a great future before you, a great future. Wish I could say the same for you, sir. (*to* LORD GORING.) But your career will have to be entirely domestic.

LORD GORING
Yes, father, I prefer it domestic.

LORD CAVERSHAM
And if you don't make this young lady an ideal husband, I'll cut you off with a shilling.

MABEL CHILTERN
An ideal husband! Oh, I don't think I should like that. It sounds like something in the next world.

LORD CAVERSHAM
What do you want him to be then, my dear?

MABEL CHILTERN
He can be what he chooses. All I want is to be . . . to be . . . oh! a real wife to him.

LORD CAVERSHAM
Upon my word, there is a good deal of common sense in that, Lady Chiltern.

They all go out except SIR ROBERT CHILTERN. *He sinks into a chair, wrapped in thought. After a little time* LADY CHILTERN *returns to look for him*

LADY CHILTERN (*leaning over the back of the chair*)
Aren't you coming in, Robert?

SIR ROBERT CHILTERN (*taking her hand*)
Gertrude, is it love you feel for me, or is it pity merely?

LADY CHILTERN (*kisses him*)

It is love, Robert. Love, and only love. For both of us a new life is beginning.

CURTAIN